THE HOME COCKTAIL BOOK FOR BEGINNERS

A COMPLETE MIXOLOGIST GUIDE WITH OVER 120 COCKTAIL RECIPES TO MASTER THE TECHNIQUES AND TOOLS OF COCKTAIL

Jerry D. McCary

Copyrights©2021 By Jerry D. McCary

All Rights Reserved

This book is copyright protected. It is only for personal use. You cannot amend, distribute, sell, use, quote or paraphrase any part of the content within this book, without the consent of the author or publisher.

Under no circumstances will any blame or legal responsibility be held against the publisher, or author, for any damages, reparation, or monetary loss due to the information contained within this book, either directly or indirectly.

Paperback ISBN: 979-8781586745

Hardcover ISBN: 979-8781592364

CONTENT

INTRODUCTION 1

Chapter 1: Bartending 101 2

Chapter 2: Learning the Art of Mixology 7

Chapter 3: Excelling at What You Do! 12

Chapter 4: Refreshing Cocktails 15

Chapter 5: Holiday Drinks 19

Chapter 6: Whiskey Drinks 25

Chapter 7: Rum Cocktails 28

Chapter 8: Mojito Cocktails 32

Chapter 9: Martini Drinks 36

Chapter 10: Cocktail Punch 40

Chapter 11: Vodka Drinks 45

Chapter 12: For the Love of Wines 50

Chapter 13: Gin Drinks 54

Chapter 14: Fruity Cocktails 60

Chapter 15: Special Cocktails 67

CONCLUSION 74

Appendix : Measurement Conversion Chart 75

INTRODUCTION

Cocktails have become an important part of our culinary culture, from parties to summer brunches, holidays and a hangout with friends- everything becomes more fun when celebrated with a glass of cocktail. There are endless varieties of alcoholic and non-alcoholic drinks that we love to enjoy, and every season, setting and mood call for a different cocktail. And the bartender is the ones that make sure to meet all your cocktails needs; that is why becoming one requires a good understanding of cocktail making, mixing and serving, along with great communication skills. And to offer you all that is a complete package, I present you my collection of cocktail recipes along with some basic bartending 101 guide to help you master the art of mixology in your personal capacity.

Bartending 101

Bartending is a profession that calls for the mastering of many skills. It is not just about pouring and serving! A bartender has to communicate well with the consumers, listen to them, make signature drinks based on the mood of the day and manage the whole bar inventory as per the cocktails served on the menu. And if you are planning to become a bartender or want to at least practise it at home- then here comes a quick and brief guide that will help you know the challenges you will be facing and the ways to deal with them with knowledge and understanding.

What to Know About Cocktails

Cocktails are mixed alcoholic drinks that are usually brightly colored and adorned with appealing garnishes. A cocktail shaker is the first and most important piece of equipment you will need as a bartender. Any jar with a sealable cover that holds at least 18 ounces of liquid will also suffice if you don't have a cocktail shaker. You will need a measuring cup to measure the cocktail components, which is also known as a jigger. With these basic things, you can start practising the mixing techniques that will be shared in the next chapter of this book.

Types of Cocktails

Depending on the type of ingredients used, the serving styles and the origin, cocktails are divided into different categories. Following are some of the major types of cocktails that every wannabe bartender must know about:

- **Margarita**

It would not be incorrect to say that Margarita is the most popular drink in America. A pitcher of margaritas is a must-have for every party or celebration. They are widely available in most US regions, with the exception of Chicago, where margaritas do not even reach the top five drink list. Margaritas are interesting in that they cost around 50 cents more than the average cocktail price in the country, but they are still quite popular and in high demand. As a result, every bartender, even a novice, should be able to produce margaritas. It's an afternoon or evening drink, so make sure you're ready to create some margaritas around that time.

- **Martini**

Martinis are one of the easiest cocktails to mix, in my opinion. So, if you're looking to improve your cocktail-making talents, this is the place to start. They're not only simple to make but also surprisingly popular. On the list of popular cocktails in the United States, this drink is second only to margaritas. The martini, unlike margaritas, is a nighttime cocktail, so have all of the ingredients ready about that time. It was first created in 1863, and since then, the drink has grown in popularity throughout time. Do you want to learn how to create a traditional martini? Then here's a quick and easy recipe to try out. Remember that the martini isn't only about the taste; it's also about the presentation, so make sure you're using the correct martini glasses and olive garnishes to give your clients the finest experience possible.

- **Old Fashioned**

Old fashioned is one of the oldest cocktails, as its name implies. W¬hen there were no other cocktails available centuries ago, this drink was there. The old-fashioned cocktail was made with bitters, sugar, spirits, and water in 1806 and was recognized as a concoction of bitters, sugar, spirits, and water. Whatever was made from a combination of spirits, water, sugar, and bitters was considered a drinkable concoction; however, it was not referred to as "old fashioned" back then. For a variety of flavour, this base mixture of ingredients was sometimes blended with rye, brandy, or bourbon. People began asking for the old drinks by requesting "old-fashioned" drinks, and the moniker evolved through time.

- **Mimosa**

It is the fourth most popular cocktail in the United States, and it is most commonly consumed in the morning or afternoon, which is unsurprising given its contents. It was created by a bartender working at the Ritz in Paris in 1925. Some people believe it was invented in the 20th century in the Mediterranean. The combination of orange juice with sparkling wine, on the other hand, was well-known among Spaniards. So, while the true origin of this cocktail is unknown, the following recipe will allow you to recreate those authentic mimosa flavors. Because the orange juice and garnishing give the drink a mimosa-like tint, the name is derived from the name of a yellow-flowering shrub.

- **Cosmopolitan**

The cosmopolitan cocktail is a relatively new drink, having been created in 1987 by Toby Cecchini of Manhattan's Odeon Restaurant. In the 1930s, there was another cocktail with a similar recipe, but this one used raspberry syrup instead of cranberry juice. There is no single known origin for this cocktail; numerous myths abound, but the current version of the cosmopolitan cocktail, which comprises the following basic ingredients, rose to popularity in the 1990s.

- **Bloody Mary**

The name "bloody Mary" is derived from Queen Mary I of England; however, some suggest it was derived from the name of a Hollywood actress, Mary Pickford, or the girlfriends of a person who ran a pub called Bucket of Blood. Whatever the cocktail's inspiration or origin is, one thing is certain: it has a distinct colour, appearance, and taste. The cocktail has a fiery flavour and is served with a variety of culinary garnishes. On the side, olives or shrimp skewers will be supplied with the cocktail. To adjust the drink's heat level, reduce or increase the amount of hot sauce used.

- **Daiquiri**

The Daiquiri is one of the most distinguished cocktails, having been named one of the "six essential drinks" in the world's most famous cocktail book, the Fine Art of Mixing Drinks, published in 1948. The drink's name was inspired by Daiquiri Beach, which contained an iron mine where an American engineer came up with the traditional idea of blending rum with citrus juice to form a refreshing beverage.

- **Whiskey Sour**

If there is one bourbon cocktail to serve in the summer, it is the whiskey sour! A Waukesha Plain merchant originated the drink in the state of Wisconsin around 1870. The sour cocktails are a whole family of drinks that are made with some of the oldest mixology techniques. All sours have the same fundamental formula: base alcohol, sour mixer, and sweetness. The rose's lime juiced in this cocktail is not lime juice but rather a sweetened sour mixer- a lime cordial. Gimlet is another sour drink.

- **Highball Drinks**

Highball cocktails are tall blended beverages that may be made quickly and easily. If you're just getting started in the bartending business, here is the place to start. These drinks are known as highballs because they are served in a Collins or highball glass. It begins with a basic liquor and is then topped with two or more mixers, such as soda or juice. "Pour and serve" beverages are what they're called.

- **Lowball Drinks**

The lowball beverages are poured into a lowball or old-fashioned glasses and served over ice or on the rocks. They're produced with a single liquor and one or more mixers. Coffee liqueur or amaretto are two liqueurs that are widely used in lowballs. These beverages are more concentrated and have a stronger flavour than highball cocktails because they are offered in small quantities. Most lowball drinks have nearly identical formulas, so be careful while making one because a small adjustment in an ingredient can completely modify the drink.

Serving Drinks and Cocktails

Pouring out in style and serving the drink at the stand is the major part of a bartender's job. Here is what you need to do to serve drinks and cocktails like a pro:

Do not re-use the ice in the cocktail shaker. You'll dilute the cocktail if you don't shake it. When utilizing ice produced by an ITV machine with crisp and compact ice cubes, you can use the mixing glass a maximum of two times. This is true when creating the same cocktail; but, if you're mixing a different one, you should always change the ice.

Never shake fizzy drinks; if you do, you'll have a bomb on your hands with a delayed fuse.

If the drinks contain fruit juice, add the sugar right away, mix it in with the juice, and then add the rest of the ingredients: eggs, creams, and liquors. Then add the ice: five or six ice cubes should suffice. Don't mix more than three mixes at a time, and don't swamp the main body content with them.

Fill the mixing glass halfway with ice and swish the ice cubes about with a spoon for 15 to 20 seconds; this will cool the glass and prevent the ice cubes from leaping around when you add liquid. Use a cocktail strainer to drain all the water content after swishing the ice around. Incorporate the liquors in descending sequence of density.

Shake elegantly, remembering to go up and down, forward and backwards for 10 to 25 seconds, depending on the cocktail you're creating. You'll notice the metal's chilly temperature, which indicates that it's ready. Don't overfill the shaker or the cocktail glass to ensure a proper mix.

When presenting Cocktails, fill them on a scale of less to more, then fill them in the opposite manner, from more to less: this will ensure that the Cocktails are aesthetically, as well as in flavour and temperature, equal.

Serve the cocktails right away: as seen in many movies, leaving the cocktail shaker on the table and serving as you go doesn't work. The cocktail will become diluted if left in the shaker, and the ingredients will not be properly blended.

Once the cocktails are ready, place them on a tray covered with a cloth to prevent spilling and serve them to your guests with care. Always serve women first and from their right side, according to serving standards.

When presenting Cocktails, fill them on a scale of less to more, then fill them in the opposite manner, from more to less: this will ensure that the Cocktails are aesthetically, as well as in flavour and temperature, equal.

If you have room in the freezer, you may store your cocktail glasses inside (don't do this if they're made of really fine crystal since they'll break), so they'll be chilled when you serve. Make room for a bottle of gin and another bottle of vodka; your Martinis will be excellent.

Understanding Liquor and Liqueur

- **Liquors**

Liquors are the strong-flavoured alcohol-based cocktail ingredients that are essential items for every bar inventory. There are an endless variety of liquors, and they are available in different bottle sizes and under different brand labels. Here is a complete basic list of all the liquors that a bartender must have in his inventory.

- Beer
- Bourbon
- Brandy/Cognac
- Champagne
- Dry/Sweet Vermouth
- Gin
- Irish Cream
- light/dark rum
- Rye/Canadian
- Scotch
- Tequila
- Vodka
- Whiskey
- White (dry)
- Wine

- **Liqueurs**

Liqueurs are just as important to a well-stocked bar because they provide taste to beverages. Liqueurs are available in practically every flavour imaginable, ranging from sweetened fruits, chocolate, or coffee to sharp spices and special blends like Benedictine and Chartreuse that are really one-of-a-kind.

CHAPTER 2

Learning the Art of Mixology

Cocktail making is not a random act of mixing spirits, juice and other ingredients! There are multiple steps, tricks, and techniques involved in this process. Though every drink has a unique recipe of its own, there are some general methods of mixing, pouring, and serving a cocktail. Every wannabe bartender must start by learning those techniques and then practice them. In this chapter, I will be discussing all cocktails making and techniques required to do so!

What is Mixology?

Mixology is the science of preparing drinks by bringing different ingredients together in a way that their taste starts complementing one another. You cannot make a martini by adding tomato juice to it- it is only suitable for making a shot of bloody Mary. Similarly, there are a lot of garnishes that only go well with certain drinks, like a pineapple ring does not complement the taste of a White Russian cocktail; it is only suitable to garnish a pine colada or a refreshing Mojito. That's what mixology is about- knowing the taste of the cocktail ingredients and mixing them in perfect proportions, and that's the forte of every bartender that he must know the secrets of mixology.

Different Ways of Preparing a Cocktail

Cocktail making involves a series of steps. Besides mixing and shaking- which I will come to later, there are multiple preparation techniques involved, which we will discuss in this section.

1. **Muddling**

Muddling means crushing or lightly blending some ingredients together before adding to the cocktail. Muddling is employed to press and release the flavors and juices out of certain ingredients so that they would give a stronger flavor to drink. There are a variety of ingredients that are muddled to prepare different cocktails, and the list includes some fruits, lemon, lime, or orange wedges, ginger slices, some spices, and fresh herbs.

2. **Building**

The building is not really a technique, rather it is a term that is associated with the process of making a drink, but it is important to talk about building while talking about the art of cocktail making. In bartending lingo, building means preparing a drink by pouring its ingredients into the serving glass or glasses.

3. **Straining**

Straining is another technique that is used to remove the solids from the drinks. Some ingredients have great flavors, but they don't taste good when let in the drink, so they are strained before the cocktail is poured into the serving glasses. The ingredients that are strained include blended fruits, herbs, pulp, ice cubes, or ice shards.

4. **Layering**

It is one of the basic bartending techniques, and it is used to make plenty of colorful and appealing drinks. The technique makes use of the natural densities of the cocktail liquors. Layering gives a cocktail a nice and elegant look.

5. **Flaming**

The flaming technique is for highly skilled bartenders and who practice flaming under some supervision. This is not just a cool presentation technique for spectacles, but it is actually used to infuse some strong flavors into a drink. To light up a drink, a bartender needs to add some inflammable liquor on top with a spoon.

6. **Rolling**

Rolling is another mixing technique. It comes in between the stirring and shaking techniques because it mixes the ingredients more thoroughly than the stirring technique, yet it mixes more gently than the shaking technique. This technique works best when you don't want to over dilute the drink, but you still want to mix them a little.

7. Blending

Blending is a simple mixing of different ingredients of a drink. Keep in mind that the blend is different from shaking because when you blend the ingredients together, they are pureed in a blended mixture, which is not the case with shaking. Blending is more commonly used for drinks and cocktails, which have herbs, cream, and fruits, etc.

8. Garnishing

Garnishing is one last step to make the cocktail look ravishing and irresistible. Some garnishes are merely for presentation, whereas others are added for taste, aroma, and presentation.

Mixing Techniques and Cocktail Shakers

Among all the drink-making techniques, the following are the ones that are most used and require the most of your attention and practice. Here is how you put your cocktails shakers to good use:

1. Shaking

Shaking is the most popular method, and most of the quick-serve cocktails are made by shaking the contents together in a cocktail shaker or other suitable container. To make a shaken drink, combine all of the ingredients in a cocktail shaker. Junior bartenders must measure the correct amounts of the ingredients before pouring them into the shaker, whereas experienced bartenders can pour the liquids directly from their bottles. If necessary, add ice, then cover the shaker with its lid or the tin. Hold the shaker in both hands and keep the end away from the clients. Then violently shake for at least 15 seconds up and down. Then, using the palm of your hand, tap the top of the cocktail shaker, then remove the tin.

2. Dry Shaking

There's also "dry shaking," which is a different form of shaking. When thick materials such as cream or egg whites are included in the drinks, this approach is used. As a result, when they're shaken, a thick foam form in the drink. You don't put the ice in the shaker with the other ingredients in this procedure. After vigorously shaking all of the components together, the ice is added to the prepared cocktail. You won't lose the thick froth that forms on top while shaking this method. There are bartenders that strain the cocktail through a hawthorn strainer while keeping the shaker at a suitable distance from the glass to increase the amount of foam in the drink. But that is entirely optional; a dry-shake will suffice to produce decent foam.

3. Stirring

Another approach to mixing the cocktail components is to stir them. Martinis are often made with a stirring technique. Because this approach is less violent than shaking, it is typically used for prepared drinks that do not require foam on top. Clear drinks and basic liquids are the most commonly stirred. As a result, once the liquids have been blended together, the drink can be served without any straining, either simple or double.

Here's how you get started with stirring! Fill the mixing glass halfway with ice, then fill it halfway with a metal rod or a bar spoon. Pour in all of the liquids and other ingredients, then stir with the spoon for 30 seconds while holding the stem between your two fingers. A bartender is claimed to whisk the components for as long as it takes for a bite of alcohol to disappear in the back of the throat, which is nearly 30 seconds.

Knowing Your Ingredients

Making a perfect drink is all about mixing ingredients that complement one another. So, unless you don't know your ingredients, you won't be able to make a perfect drink. Following are some basic ingredients that every bartender must be well familiar with. Every spirit and fruit juice taste different, so they must be used differently.

1. **Rum**

However, for those classic cocktails that are requested time and time again, you'll only need three basic ingredients, with the occasional garnish or filler thrown in for good measure. Rum that is white in colour White rum is a versatile spirit that is used as the base component in several popular cocktails, including the Mojito and the Daiquiri. A basic Daiquiri is a winner in and of itself, but if you can provide your guests with a variety of flavour selections, they'll be wowed.

2. **Vodka**

Vodka is still a popular spirit in the United States, and with good reason. The simplest of cocktails, from the traditional Cosmopolitan or Moscow Mule to a more complicated Bloody Mary or Espresso Martini, may be made using a vodka base.

3. **Whiskey**

With two light liquors on hand, you'll want to add two dark liquors for a full range of cocktail options. Whiskey is an easy pick because it's used in so many popular cocktails, including the Manhattan and the Whiskey Sour, which are two of the best-selling cocktails on the list.

4. **Dark Rum**

Dark rum cocktails are less popular than white rum cocktails, but there are lots of great drink recipes that make us question why. The first is the Old Fashioned, which is currently the most popular cocktail among drinkers. For those who prefer a little extra richness, a black rum Daiquiri and a calm and soothing Mai Tai are also available.

5. **Maple Syrup**

Syrup is a sweet ingredient that can be found in a variety of drinks, including Whiskey Sour, Vodka Sour, Mojito, and many more. It's a handy ingredient to have for making cocktails, and you can simply make it yourself with only sugar and water.

6. **Lime slices for juice and garnish**

Cocktails are normally balanced with one sweet and one sour ingredient. Lime juice is a classic sour component that can be squeezed directly into the cocktail or purchased ready to serve. It works because lime lowers the alcohol flavour, making the cocktail simpler to drink while also bringing out the flavour in a cocktail, such as the Margarita. Fresh limes are, of course, a frequent garnish for cocktails, so they're necessary even if you don't need the juice.

7. **Oranges for garnish and juice**

One of the most flexible cocktail ingredients is fruit juice. Tomato juice, for a killer Bloody Mary, and cranberry juice are two lesser-known but crucial ingredients infamous cocktails like Cosmopolitan or Sex on the Beach. With this in mind, you might want to go all out and stock three or four mixers.

8. Carbonated water

Simple soda water is a wonderful filler for many cocktails and can really give your drink that extra touch of refreshing. The benefit of soda water is that it can be readily added to otherwise simple mixed beverages, such as vodka and orange juice, to provide a delightful fizz.

9. Ice

Although it may seem apparent, ice is a must-have cocktail ingredient that you will never want to run out of! Keep your freezer supplied with crushed ice for Daiquiris or cubes of ice for numerous cocktails and mixed drinks, and you'll always be ready to mix.

10. Mint

Mint is an extra garnish that will nearly always come in handy if you've already stocked up on limes and oranges. A mint-topped drink, especially in the warmer months, is extremely delightful; just think of the Mojito! Furthermore, mint can be added to your simple syrup to give classic mixed drinks like vodka soda an extra flavour boost.

11. Gin

Gin is becoming more popular as a spirit, so carrying both vodka and gin will ensure that you cover all of your bases when it comes to serving cocktails.

12. Pineapple juice

For classics like the Pina Colada or for blending with juice-based drinks, pineapple juice is a healthy and refreshing addition, so have it in your inventory.

CHAPTER 3

Excelling at What You Do!

Let's say you have all ingredients at your disposal, and you learned about all the mixing techniques and garnishing styles, can that make you a successful bartender? It always take time and practice to master the job you are want to work for. So don't be disheartened if you mess up a few drinks or just can't pour right- just be consistent with your efforts and see how it magically improves your skills.

Special Tips and Techniques for Bartenders:

There are certain techniques that every experienced and seasoned bartender follows, and if you too follow in their footsteps, that will help you in the long run. Here are a few simple yet very useful techniques that every wannabe bartender must keep in mind while practising his skills.

1. *Know your cocktail.*

In a cocktail glass, each base liquor has a distinct purpose. Great vodka should be flavorless, so it may be used with everything from vermouth to orange juice in a Martini (in a Screwdriver). When blended into a Martini or a Tom Collins, gin is made from juniper berries and should retain its unique flavour. Whiskey and rye have a smokey flavour that lingers on the roof of a drinker's mouth. They're fantastic in drinks like Manhattans and Old Fashioned since they're hearty. Rum is sweeter than most other liquors and is the main component in Dark 'N' Storms and Daiquiris. It can be dark or clear. Succulents are used to make tequila and mezcal, which pair well with citrus flavors in beverages like Margaritas.

2. *Master the art of the free pour.*

A jigger is a measuring tool used by experienced bartenders to pour precise amounts of spirits into mixing glasses. A free pour involves tilting the bottle and pouring liquor into the glass without using a measuring device. Both pouring techniques should be familiar to a great bartender.

3. *Learn how to make a cocktail shake.*

Shaking is the standard method of mixing non-carbonated beverages like Mojitos, Whiskey Sours, and the French 75 in many establishments. Purchasing your own cocktail shaker is a must. Some shakers come with lids, while others, such as the Boston shaker, resemble two tin cups joined together. You'll also need to learn how to make a thick foam with materials like cream and egg whites using the dry shake.

4. *Learn how to make a drink by stirring it.*

Some cocktails, such as a Manhattan, a Sidecar on the rocks, and, yes, even a Martini, require stirring. Any spoon can be used to stir a drink, but an extra-long bar spoon is specifically created for this function. A swizzle stick can also be used.

5. *Layering is a skill worth learning.*

A talented bartender can layer drinks such that you can see layers of different liquids within the glassware in addition to shaking and stirring. A bar spoon is required, as well as knowledge of how to layer liqueurs, fruit liquids, egg whites, foam, and other drink ingredients as needed.

6. *Muddling is a good thing to do.*

A muddler is a long stick that is used to smash items like mint, ginger, and citrus peel. Think of it as a cocktail pestle. Many of the most exquisite mixed drinks go beyond just liquid ingredients. You'll need to know how to muddle to make them properly.

7. *Drinks should be strained appropriately.*

When you wish to avoid ice cubes, ice shards, or particles of fresh ingredients from going into the cocktail glass, strain the drink. The majority of professional bartenders have a collection of strainers. Using a Hawthorn strainer to remove coarser materials and then a fine strainer to remove microscopic bits of fruit or ice is the double-strain technique. A common double-strained drink is the Cosmopolitan. Meanwhile, a strainer dedicated to Mint Juleps has been created: the Julep strainer.

8. *Make a list of cocktail recipes to remember.*

You don't have to know everything, but knowing some classic cocktails by memory is part of bartending 101. You should be able to make a Bloody Mary, a Martini (with dry vermouth), a Margarita (with plenty of lime juice), a Vodka Cranberry, a Gin & Tonic (try it with grapefruit juice), and a Negroni at the very least. After that, you can start learning about the different types of cocktails, such as highballs, fizzes, sours, punches, and so on. You'll have a better understanding of how to make each drink within that category once you've learned the characteristics of each category.

Frequently Asked Question

Q: Is it possible to shake beverages over ice while keeping my cocktail in the freezer?

Shaking serves two purposes: chilling and dilution. Freezing, on the other hand, does nothing but cool your drink, and without dilution, your cocktails will taste a touch too powerful. If you truly don't like ice, replace it with an ounce of super-cold water in any cocktail you prepare with your frozen alcohol. It'll be easier to dilute if you do that.

Q: What should you batch and what shouldn't you batch?

The short answer to this question is that batching is worthwhile if you intend to use it. Even the most upscale cocktail bars batch at least some of their drinks because it saves time.

Q: What's the most efficient way to make a large number of cocktails at once? Would I just throw everything into a pitcher and whisk it?

You could do it if you were creating a pitcher of Negronis, but I wouldn't encourage it. Because once you've finished stirring your massive cocktail, all of the ice cubes you used to mix it will still be in the pitcher, destined for a silent, watery death (while diluting your cocktail). So, ideally, you'll whisk everything together in your pitcher before transferring it to a pitcher with fresh ice.

Q: What are your thoughts on the use of soda in cocktails?

I used to bring things into work to experiment with all the time when I worked as a bartender. Cream soda, orange soda, and root beer were among the beverages included. And with all of that, I prepared some tasty cocktails. So go ahead and experiment with some soda. Just make sure it's not completely flat.

Q: What are the ideal ingredients for Cosmopolitans?

I've been getting a lot of queries lately about Cosmos. Perhaps they're making a comeback. Or perhaps they never departed in the first place. In any case, a Cosmopolitan has four characteristics: triple sec, citron vodka, lime juice, and cranberry juice.

CHAPTER 4

Refreshing Cocktails

Refreshing Pina Colada	16
Sparkling Mint Cocktail	16
Gooseberry and Elderflower Fizz with Lemon	17
Summer Cocktail-Long Island Iced Tea Cocktail	17
Refreshing Summer Cocktail	17
Classic Refreshing Mint Julep	17
Lime Daiquiri	18
Waterloo Sunset Cocktail	18
Refreshing Sex on The Beach Cocktail	18

Refreshing Pina Colada

Prep Time: 5 minutes, Cook Time: 0, Serves: 1

INGREDIENTS:

120ml fresh pineapple juice

60ml coconut cream

60ml white rum

A handful of ice cubes

A slice of pineapple for decoration

DIRECTIONS:

1. Add all the ingredients into a regular blender, apart from the decorative pineapple.
2. Blitz the mixture until a smooth consistency occurs.
3. Pour the mixture into a tall cocktail glass.
4. Decorate with the slice of pineapple.

Sparkling Mint Cocktail

Prep Time: 15 minutes, Cook Time: 20 minutes, Serves: 4

INGREDIENTS:

85g golden caster sugar

4 tbsps. fresh lemon juice

1 bottle of sparkling wine

Fresh mint

DIRECTIONS:

1. In a saucepan, heat sugar and lemon juice. Simmer until you get a syrupy texture.
2. Take six Champagne flutes, pour the lemon syrup into them.
3. Top up with sparkling wine.
4. Add mint leaves for decoration.

Gooseberry and Elderflower Fizz with Lemon

Prep Time: 15 minutes, Cook Time: 0, Serves: 1

INGREDIENTS:

1 tbsp. caster sugar	cordial
12 gooseberries	The juice ½ lemon
3 tbsps. elderflower	Prosecco

DIRECTIONS:

1. Take a large jar, add sugar and gooseberries into it. Mash the mixture down into a pulp.
2. Add cordial, lemon juice, and ice cubes. Close the jar lid and shake well.
3. Take a glass, pour the mixture into it and top up with the Prosecco before serving.

Refreshing Summer Cocktail

Prep Time: 5 minutes, Cook Time: 0, Serves: 1

INGREDIENTS:

A handful of ice cubes	A large cucumber, cut into long slices
2 tbsps. gin	
A handful of coriander	A little tonic water to serve

DIRECTIONS:

1. Take a tumbler glass, add a few ice cubes, gin and a few sprigs of the coriander.
2. Place a slice of cucumber into the glass to act as a stirrer.
3. Top up with the glass with your desired amount of tonic water.
4. Combine the mixtures and enjoy.

Summer Cocktail-Long Island Iced Tea Cocktail

Prep Time: 15 minutes, Cook Time: 0, Serves: 4

INGREDIENTS:

50ml vanilla vodka	50ml fresh lime juice
50ml rum	500ml cola
50ml London dry gin	Ice cubes
50ml tequila	2 limes, cut into wedges
50ml triple sec	

DIRECTIONS:

1. Take a large jug, pour all the spirits and liqueurs into it.
2. Add lime juice, fill ½ of the jug with ice cubes and stir well.
3. Add cola and stir once again.
4. Take 4 tall glasses, pour the cocktail into it and add extra ice cubes.
5. Decorate with lime wedges.

Classic Refreshing Mint Julep

Prep Time: 5 minutes, Cook Time: 0, Serves: 1

INGREDIENTS:

65ml bourbon	Crushed ice
12.5ml sugar syrup	10 fresh mint leaves
A handful of ice cubes	

DIRECTIONS:

1. Take a cocktail shaker, add the bourbon, sugar syrup, mint, and ice cubes, combining well.
2. Take a highball glass, add crushed ice.
3. Strain the cocktail into the glass.
4. Churn the cocktail by moving it around quickly inside the glass with a long-handled spoon.
5. Add a little more crushed ice and serve with a straw.

Lime Daiquiri

Prep Time: 10 minutes, Cook Time: 0, Serves: 1

INGREDIENTS:

50ml white rum

25ml lime juice

10ml sugar syrup

Ice cubes

DIRECTIONS:

1. Take a cocktail shaker, put rum, lime juice, and sugar syrup into it. Shake well.
2. Take a glass, strain the cocktail into it and add extra ice cubes.

Waterloo Sunset Cocktail

Prep Time: 10 minutes, Cook Time: 0, Serves: 8

INGREDIENTS:

200ml vanilla flavoured vodka	A little grenadine to taste
500ml peach juice, chilled	A little lemonade
100ml schnapps, peach works best for this cocktail	A handful of fresh or frozen raspberries
	A handful of ice cubes

DIRECTIONS:

1. In a mixing jug, add vodka, juice, and schnapps into it, and stir well.
2. Pour the cocktail into 8 glasses.
3. Add a few ice cubes to each glass, then pour lemonade.
4. Pour a teaspoon of syrup into the glass.
5. Garnish with raspberries.

Refreshing Sex on The Beach Cocktail

Prep Time: 10 minutes, Cook Time: 0, Serves: 2

INGREDIENTS:

50ml cranberry juice	Ice cubes
The juice of 2 oranges	Glacé cherries to garnish
50ml vodka	
25ml peach schnapps	Orange slices, to garnish

DIRECTIONS:

1. Take a large jug, pour the fruit juices, vodka, and peach schnapps into it. Stir the mixtures until they are well mixed together.
2. Take two glasses, fill the glasses with the ice cubes and pour the mixture into them. Stir once again.
3. Add cherries and additional orange slices for decoration.

CHAPTER 5

Holiday Drinks

Simple Cosmopolitan Cocktail	20
Homemade Bloody Mary Cocktail	20
Sazerac Cognac Cocktail	21
Old St. Nick Cocktail	21
Manhattan Cocktail	21
Chocolate Mudslide Cocktail	21
Easy White Russian Cocktail	22
Homemade Gimlet	22
Sweet Vermouth Cocktail	22
Refreshing Creamy Bourbon	23
Easy Frozen Margarita	23
Stormy Coffee Cocktail	24
Mint And Dark Chocolate	24
White Russian Cocktail	24
Perfect Margarita Cocktail	24

Simple Cosmopolitan Cocktail

Prep Time: 5 minutes, Cook Time: 0, Serves: 2

INGREDIENTS:

45ml (1.5 oz.(42 g)) lemon vodka

30ml (1 oz.) cranberry juice

10ml (0.33 oz.(9.3 g)) lime juice

15ml (0.5 oz.(14g)) triple sec

Ora zest or lime wedge, to garnish

Ice

DIRECTIONS:

1. Take a cocktail shaker, add all ingredients into it, and shake the mixtures with abundant ice.
2. Take a cocktail glass, pour the drink into it.
3. For decoration, waving a slice of orange peel on a lighted match. Bend the outer edge of the zest toward the flame to release all the orange essential oil. After a few seconds, drop the zest into the cocktail.

Homemade Bloody Mary Cocktail

Prep Time: 10 minutes, Cook Time: 0, Serves: 1

INGREDIENTS:

50ml vodka

1 tsp. sherry vinegar

2 tbsps. amontillado sherry

200ml tomato juice

Ice cubes

Tabasco, to taste

A pinch of salt

Worcestershire sauce, to taste

Lemon juice

Celery sticks

Lemon wedges

DIRECTIONS:

1. Take a tall glass, pour the vodka, sherry vinegar, amontillado and tomato juice into it along with some ice cubes.
2. Season with Tabasco, celery salt, Worcestershire sauce and lemon juice.
3. Decorate with lemon wedges and celery sticks.

Sazerac Cognac Cocktail

Prep Time: 20 minutes, Cook Time: 0, Serves: 1

INGREDIENTS:

- 2 drops of absinthe
- 30ml cognac
- 30ml rye whiskey
- 2 drops of Peychaud's bitters
- 5ml ugar syrup
- Lemon peel

DIRECTIONS:

1. Refrigerate a tumbler. After cooling, pour the absinthe into it.
2. Take a mixing glass, pour all the remaining ingredients into it, apart from the lemon zest. Stir well and pour into the tumbler.
3. Add lemon zest for decoration.

Manhattan Cocktail

Prep Time: 10 minutes, Cook Time: 0, Serves: 1

INGREDIENTS:

- 50ml bourbon
- 25ml Rosso vermouth
- 25ml syrup for a jar of maraschino cherries
- 2 dashes Angostura bitters
- Ice cubes
- Maraschino cherries to garnish

DIRECTIONS:

1. Take a mixing glass, add all ingredients and a few ice cubes in it, stir well.
2. Take a glass, pour the cocktail into it, decorate with additional maraschino cherries.

Old St. Nick Cocktail

Prep Time: 15 minutes, Cook Time: 0, Serves: 2

INGREDIENTS:

- 200ml cognac
- 150ml muscat wine
- 120ml double cream
- 60ml simple syrup
- 6 egg whites
- Ice cubes
- 6 cloves
- 6 strips of orange peel
- Ground cinnamon

DIRECTIONS:

1. Take a cocktail shaker and combine 1/3 of the ingredients, apart from the cloves, orange peel, and cinnamon.
2. Take two wine glasses, pour the mixture into them.
3. Repeat with the remaining 2/3 of the ingredients, adding fresh ice cubes each time.
4. Add cloves, peeled oranges, and a little cinnamon to each glass for decoration.

Chocolate Mudslide Cocktail

Prep Time: 15 minutes, Cook Time: 10 minutes, Serves: 1

INGREDIENTS:

- 50g dark chocolate
- 60ml vodka
- 60ml Irish cream liqueur
- 60ml coffee-flavoured liqueur
- 100ml double cream
- Ice cubes

DIRECTIONS:

1. Microwave half of the dark chocolate.
2. Chill two small glasses. Immerse the rim of the cup in the melted chocolate, then put them back in the refrigerator.
3. Take a cocktail shaker, add vodka, liqueur, double cream, and ice cubes into it. Shake well.
4. Add extra ice cubes to the chilled glasses, then pour the cocktail.
5. Sprinkle extra chocolate chips on top.

Easy White Russian Cocktail

Prep Time: 10 minutes, Cook Time: 0, Serves: 1

INGREDIENTS:

60ml vodka

2 tbsps. Kahlua

1 tbsp. cream

Ice cubes

DIRECTIONS:

1. Take a mixing jug, put the vodka, Kahlua, and cream into it. Stir the mixtures until they are well mixed together.
2. Take a small tumbler, add extra ice cubes and serve.

Homemade Gimlet

Prep Time: 10 minutes, Cook Time: 0, Serves: 1

INGREDIENTS:

50ml lime syrup or lime cordial

Ice cubes

50ml London dry gin

1 slice of lime, to garnish

1 edible flower, to garnish

DIRECTIONS:

1. Leave a coupe glass in the refrigerator to cool down for a while.
2. Take a tall glass, pour lime syrup or cordial into it, add some ice cubes.
3. Add gin and stir well.
4. Pour the mixture into the chilled glass.
5. Add a slice of lime and an edible flower for decoration.

Sweet Vermouth Cocktail

Prep Time: 15 minutes, Cook Time: 0, Serves: 1

INGREDIENTS:

420g canned peaches with syrup, cut into thin slices

1 orange, sliced

1 banana, sliced

1 pear, sliced

1 lemon, sliced

1 bottle red wine

200ml sweet red vermouth

200ml lemonade

Ice cubes

Lemon and orange slices

DIRECTIONS:
1. Combine all the fruits and syrup in a mixing bowl. Stir well with a wooden spoon.
2. Add the absinthe and red wine, mix again.
3. Add ice cubes and lemonade, stir well.
4. Add lemon slices and orange slices for decoration.

Refreshing Creamy Bourbon

Prep Time: 5 minutes, Cook Time: 0, Serves: 2

INGREDIENTS:

4 tbsps. bourbon

4 tbsps. fresh lemon juice

4 tbsps. creme de cacao

4 tsps. caster sugar

A handful of ice cubes

A little orange zest for decoration

DIRECTIONS:
1. Take a cocktail shaker, add all the ingredients into it.
2. Shake to combine, until the outside of the shaker is cold.
3. Pour the cocktail into two martini glasses.
4. Decorate with zest and serve.

Easy Frozen Margarita

Prep Time: 10 minutes, Cook Time: 0, Serves: 1

INGREDIENTS:

50ml tequila

25ml Cointreau

25ml lime juice

15ml sugar syrup

Ice cubes

A couple of wedges of lime, to garnish

DIRECTIONS:
1. Take a blender, put all the ingredients in it.
2. Shake the mixtures until smooth.
3. Take a margarita glass, pour the cocktail into it.
4. Add the lime wedges for decoration.

Stormy Coffee Cocktail

Prep Time: 10 minutes, Cook Time: 0, Serves: 1

INGREDIENTS:

Ice cubes

25ml tequila

25ml dark rum

Ginger beer

2 tbsps. freshly brewed espresso

DIRECTIONS:

1. Take a glass, fill it with ice cubes.
2. Pour in tequila and rum, top with ginger beer.
3. Pour espresso before serving.

White Russian Cocktail

Prep Time: 5 minutes, Cook Time: 0, Serves: 1

INGREDIENTS:

60ml vodka

2 tbsps. Kahlua

1 tbsp. double cream

Handful of ice cubes

DIRECTIONS:

1. Prepare a mixing jug, add vodka, Kahlua, and cream into it, and mix them together.
2. Take a tumbler glass, add a few ice cubes.
3. Pour the cocktail into the glass and enjoy whilst cold.

Mint And Dark Chocolate

Prep Time: 20 minutes, Cook Time: 15 minutes, Serves: 1

INGREDIENTS:

50ml double cream

Peppermint extract

1 tsp. icing sugar

150ml whole milk

25ml crème de menthe

50g dark chocolate, chopped

Dark chocolate sprinkles

DIRECTIONS:

1. Take a mixing bowl, add cream, peppermint extract and powdered sugar into it. Whip the mixture well. Once ready, store in the refrigerator.
2. Heat the milk to boiling. Stir often!
3. Turn off the heat and add chocolate. Stir the mixture until you get a creamy texture.
4. Reheat over medium heat and stir in the crème the menthe.
5. Take a mug, pour the mixture into it.
6. Drizzle with whipped mint cream and add dark chocolate sprinkles for decoration.
7. Serve warm and enjoy!

Perfect Margarita Cocktail

Prep Time: 15 minutes, Cook Time: 20 minutes, Serves: 4

INGREDIENTS:

5 limes, halved

Honey

1 cup tequila

½ cup Cointreau

Salt and ground chipotle chile

ice cubes

DIRECTIONS:

1. Prepare a grill. Coat the cut side of the limes with honey and place, cut side down, over medium heat until charred and soft. Squeeze the lime halves to get ½ cup juice.
2. Mix salt and chipotle in a 2:1 ratio.
3. Take four glasses, fill glasses with ice. Moisten rims of each glass with the squeezed lime juice and dip into the chipotle salt.
4. Take a cocktail shaker, add the lime juice, tequila, Cointreau, and ice cubes into it. Shake well.
5. Use a strainer to pour the mixture into prepared glasses.

CHAPTER 6

Whiskey Drinks

Easy Whiskey Sour	26
Fantastic Irish Whiskey	26
Classic Manhattan Whiskey	27
Hot whiskey Toddy	27
Essential Whiskey Cocktail	27
Classic Whiskey Old Fashioned	27

Easy Whiskey Sour

Prep Time: 10 minutes, Cook Time: 0, Serves: 2

INGREDIENTS:

A little honey

50ml bourbon

Crushed ice

1 tbsp. orange juice, fresh is best

1 tbsp. lemon juice, fresh is best

0.5 tbsp. sugar syrup

Orange slices

DIRECTIONS:

1. Take two whiskey tumblers, add a little honey to the rim of each glass.
2. Add the crushed ice equally to each glass.
3. Take a cocktail shaker, add the bourbon and the orange, lemon, and sugar syrups into it and give it a few good shakes.
4. Strain the cocktail equally into each glass.
5. A slice of orange for decoration.

Fantastic Irish Whiskey

Prep Time: 5 minutes, Cook Time: 0, Serves: 1

INGREDIENTS:

40ml Irish whiskey

10ml Sauternes

10ml elderflower (cordial)

A handful of ice cubes

A little lemon zest for decoration

DIRECTIONS:

1. Take a mixing jug, add the ingredients into it.
2. Stir carefully until everything is combined.
3. Make sure the ice cubes have melted slightly before serving.
4. Pour the cocktail into a glass.
5. Decorate with a little lemon zest.

Classic Manhattan Whiskey

Prep Time: 5 minutes, Cook Time: 0, Serves: 1

INGREDIENTS:

50ml bourbon

25ml vermouth

5ml cherry syrup

2 dashes of Angostura bitters

A handful of ice cubes

1 maraschino cherry for decoration

A twist of lemon for decoration

DIRECTIONS:

1. Take a mixing jug and add all the ingredients, except for the decorations.
2. Stir carefully until everything is combined.
3. Combine gently with a bar spoon.
4. Strain it into your serving glass.
5. Decorate with cherry and twist of lemon.

Essential Whiskey Cocktail

Prep Time: 5 minutes, Cook Time: 0, Serves: 1

INGREDIENTS:

2 tsps. sugar syrup

2 dashes of Angostura bitters

60ml bourbon

A dash of cold water

A little soda water

A handful of ice cubes

A slice of orange for decoration

DIRECTIONS:

1. Take a small tumbler, and add the sugar syrup, bitters, and cold water, combining well.
2. Take a glass, add the ice cubes and pour the whiskey over the top.
3. Add the soda water and mix carefully.
4. Decorate with a slice of orange.

Hot whiskey Toddy

Prep Time: 5 minutes, Cook Time: 0, Serves: 2

INGREDIENTS:

50 milliliters of whisky

3 tsps. honey (the best honey for this cocktail is runny honey)

Lemon juice (one lemon)

1 cinnamon stick, halved

200 milliliters of boiling water

a few lemon wedges as a finishing touch

2 garlic cloves

DIRECTIONS:

1. Combine the honey and whiskey in a small mixing jug.
2. Fill two heatproof glasses halfway with boiling water and half a cinnamon stick each.
3. Fill each glass halfway with lemon juice.
4. Add a lemon slice and a clove to each glass.

Classic Whiskey Old Fashioned

Prep Time: 10 minutes, Cook Time: 0, Serves: 1

INGREDIENTS:

2 dashes Angostura bitters

2 tsps. sugar syrup

1 splash of water

60ml Scotch whisky

Soda water

Orange slice, to garnish

Maraschino cherry, to garnish

DIRECTIONS:

1. Take a small tumbler, put the water, bitters, and sugar into it. Stir the mixtures until they are well mixed together.
2. Add whiskey and then fill the glass with ice.
3. Top the glass up with a splash of sparkling water.
4. Add he cherry on a cocktail stick and orange slice for decoration before serving.

CHAPTER 7

Rum Cocktails

Rum and Chocolate Milk	29
Homemade Spicy Rum	29
Bergamot Rum Cocktail	30
Iced Tea and Rum Cocktail	30
Coconut Rum Chocolate	30
Hurricane Rum Cocktail	30
Coconut Rum Cocktail	31
Pineapple Rum Cocktail	31

Rum and Chocolate Milk

Prep Time: 15 minutes, Cook Time: 10 minutes, Serves: 1

INGREDIENTS:

150ml whole milk

50g milk chocolate

25ml dark rum

2 tbsps. dulce de leche or thick caramel

DIRECTIONS:

1. Take a mixing jug, combine the milk juice and rum until you get a smooth cream.
2. In a saucepan, warm the milk. Add chocolate and stir well until the chocolate melts.
3. Turn on the heat again and add the rum mixture.
4. Take a cup, pour the cocktail into it and season with a bit of salt.

Homemade Spicy Rum

Prep Time: 20 minutes, Cook Time: 0, Serves: 5

INGREDIENTS:

30ml water

60g caster sugar

1 tbsp. ground allspice

200ml rum

90ml fresh lime juice

600ml champagne

A few slices of orange for decoration

DIRECTIONS:

1. Add sugar, water, and allspice to a small saucepan.
2. Stir gently over medium heat until the sugar has completely dissolved.
3. Remove the pan from the heat and let it cool completely.
4. After cooling, remove any grains of allspice from the mixture with a fine sieve.
5. Add rum, lime juice, and the strained spice mixture into a cocktail shaker. Combine the mixture by shaking vigorously.
6. Divide the mixture between 6 champagne flutes evenly, leaving a little space at the top.
7. Top up the glasses with champagne.
8. Add a slice of orange for decoration.

Bergamot Rum Cocktail

Prep Time: 20 minutes, Cook Time: 10 minutes, Serves: 1

INGREDIENTS:

300g golden caster sugar

The juice of 6 limes

12 mint leaves

The juice of 1 bergamot

150ml golden rum

The zest of 1 bergamot

DIRECTIONS:

1. Boil 1 liter of water. Stir in sugar, then cool.
2. In a food processor, blend together lime juice, mint and bergamot juice and peel.
3. Add the cooled sugar syrup and mix well. Pour into a plastic container and freeze.
4. Take a chilled cocktail glass, fill it with rum, and then pour the bergamot granita into it.

Coconut Rum Chocolate

Prep Time: 10 minutes, Cook Time: 10 minutes, Serves: 1

INGREDIENTS:

150ml whole milk

25g white chocolate, chopped

1 tsp. finely grated dark chocolate

25ml coconut-flavoured rum

1 tsp. coconut flakes

DIRECTIONS:

1. In a saucepan, warm the milk and the white chocolate. Stir well until the chocolate has melted.
2. Add the rum, stir well.
3. Take a mug, pour all the ingredients into it.
4. Add coconut flakes and serve.

Iced Tea and Rum Cocktail

Prep Time: 20 minutes, Cook Time: 0, Serves: 1

INGREDIENTS:

1 chamomile tea bag

100ml pink gin

100ml spiced rum

100ml elderflower cordial

100ml pink grapefruit juice

Ice cubes

Thyme sprigs

DIRECTIONS:

1. Brew the tea bag with boiling water and steep according to the instructions on the package.
2. Take a jug, pour the remaining ingredients into it.
3. Add ice cubes, chamomile, and tea. Stir carefully until everything is combined.
4. Add thyme sprigs for decoration.

Hurricane Rum Cocktail

Prep Time: 15 minutes, Cook Time: 0, Serves: 2

INGREDIENTS:

50ml dark rum

1 passion fruit

The juice of 1 orange

The juice of 1 lemon

2 tsps. grenadine

50ml sugar syrup

50ml white rum

2 orange slices

4 cocktail cherries

DIRECTIONS:

1. Take a cocktail shaker, put the ice and the rums into it.
2. Add the passion fruit, juice of one orange, one lemon, grenadine, and sugar syrup, then shake well.
3. Take two glasses, fill them with wine and pour the cocktail into it.
4. Add additional ice cubes, orange slices, and some cocktail cherries before serving.

Coconut Rum Cocktail

Prep Time: 15 minutes, Cook Time: 0, Serves: 2

INGREDIENTS:

50ml coconut water

25ml coconut rum

The juice of ½ lime

Ice cubes

50ml prosecco

DIRECTIONS:

1. Take a cocktail shaker, add all the ingredients into it, apart from Prosecco. Shake well.
2. Take a chilled couple of glasses, pour the cocktail into them.
3. Add prosecco and serve.

Pineapple Rum Cocktail

Prep Time: 20 minutes, Cook Time: 0, Serves: 8

INGREDIENTS:

1 pineapple

Fresh mint

8 tbsps. golden caster sugar

The juice 4 limes

400ml cachaça liqueur, or light rum

800ml pineapple juice

Crushed ice

DIRECTIONS:

1. Cut pineapple into pieces.
2. Take a pitcher, add part of the pineapple chunks, half of the mint, sugar, and lime juice into it. Smash the ingredients with a wooden spoon.
3. Add cachaça and some crushed ice.
4. Take 8 glasses, pour the drink into it and add more crushed ice.
5. Add pineapple juice.
6. Add mint sprigs and extra pineapple slices for decoration.

CHAPTER 8

Mojito Cocktails

Strawberry Mojito with Lime	33
Mojito Mocktail	33
Classic Mojito Cocktail	34
Pineapple-Mango Mojito	34
Blueberry Lemon Mojito	34
Classic Minty Mojito	34
Simple Mojito with A Twist	35
Pomegranate Mojito Mocktail	35

Strawberry Mojito with Lime

Prep Time: 10 minutes, Cook Time: 0, Serves: 4

INGREDIENTS:

10 strawberries

2 limes, chopped

350ml (11.8oz.(335.4g)) white rum

600ml (20.3 oz.(574.4g)) sparkling water

2 tbsps. granulated sugar

Ice cubes

2 mint sprigs, with leaves

Black pepper

DIRECTIONS:

1. In a jug, add strawberries, sugar, and lime into it, mix well until you get a creamy texture.
2. Add mint leaves, strawberry mixture, and some black pepper.
3. Add soda water and rum, stir well.
4. Serve with ice cubes.

Mojito Mocktail

Prep Time: 5 minutes, Cook Time: 0, Serves: 2

INGREDIENTS:

A small bunch of fresh mint

1 tbsp. caster sugar

The juice of 3 limes

A little soda water to taste

Crushed ice

DIRECTIONS:

1. Take a small bowl, add the mint and sugar, use the end of a rolling pin to muddle.
2. Take 2 tall cocktail glasses and add crushed ice to the bottom of both.
3. Pour the sugar mixture and the lime juice into each glass equally.
4. Combine the mixtures together.
5. Add a little soda water to each glass and a few extra mint leaves for decoration.

Classic Mojito Cocktail

Prep Time: 5 minutes, Cook Time: 0, Serves: 2

INGREDIENTS:

1 tsp. granulated sugar

Mint leaves

The juice of 1 lime

60ml (2 oz.(57 g)) white rum

Soda water, to taste

Mint sprig, to garnish

DIRECTIONS:

1. Take a jug, add the sugar, mint and lime juice, muddle the mixtures until the mint is completely crushed.
2. Take a tall glass, pour the mint mixture into it, along with ice cubes.
3. Pour the rum while stirring with a spoon.
4. Fill with soda water.
5. Add additional mint leaves for decoration.

Blueberry Lemon Mojito

Prep Time: 15 minutes, Cook Time: 0, Serves: 1

INGREDIENTS:

3 lemons, chopped

100g blueberries

2 tbsps. granulated sugar

2 bruised mint sprigs, with leaves

600ml sparkling water

350ml white rum

DIRECTIONS:

1. In a jar, mix lemon, blueberries, and sugar to get a syrupy mixture.
2. Add mint leaves and some ice cubes.
3. Pour in sparkling water and rum, stir the mixtures until they are well mixed together.

Pineapple-Mango Mojito

Prep Time: 10 minutes, Cook Time: 0, Serves: 1

INGREDIENTS:

50g mango, chopped

3 limes, chopped

50g pineapple pieces

2 mint sprigs

Ice cubes

150ml pineapple rum

150ml white rum

600ml sparkling water

DIRECTIONS:

1. Take a jug, put the mango, limes, and pineapple in it with the sugar, and muddle together.
2. Add the mint leaves.
3. Top with ice cubes.
4. Pour in pineapple rum and the white rum, then add some soda water.

Classic Minty Mojito

Prep Time: 5 minutes, Cook Time: 0, Serves: 1

INGREDIENTS:

1 tsp. sugar

A few fresh mint leaves

The juice of 1 lime

A handful of ice cubes

60ml white rum

A little soda water, according to your taste

DIRECTIONS:

1. Add sugar, mint leaves, and lime juice into a small jug.
2. Use a muddler to combine, carefully crushing the leaves.
3. Take a tall cocktail glass, add the muddled mixture into it.
4. Add a handful of ice cubes on top and pour rum into the glass.
5. Stir the mixtures carefully with a long bar spoon until everything is combined.
6. Add a little soda water on top.
7. Add mint leaves for decoration.

Simple Mojito with A Twist

Prep Time: 30 minutes, Cook Time: 0, Serves: 6

INGREDIENTS:

300g sugar

The juice of 6 limes

12 mint leaves

1 juiced bergamot, keep the zest also

A handful of ice cubes

1 litre of water

150ml rum

DIRECTIONS:

1. Add sugar and water into a small saucepan.
2. Bring the pan to the boil and remove from the heat, let it cool.
3. Take a blender, add juice, mint leaves, and the zest from the bergamot, combining well.
4. Add the cooled sugar syrup and combine.
5. Take a large plastic jug and pour the mixture into the refrigerator for half an hour.
6. Take a large cocktail glass and scoop the iced mixture inside.
7. Pour the rum on top and enjoy whilst still cold.

Pomegranate Mojito Mocktail

Prep Time: 10 minutes, Cook Time: 0, Serves: 8

INGREDIENTS:

3 tbsps. pomegranate seeds

A large bunch of fresh mint

2 limes but into quarters

500ml cold lemonade

1 litre of fresh pomegranate juice

A few lime slices for decoration

DIRECTIONS:

1. Take an empty ice cube tray, put the pomegranate seeds into it, add water. Place in the freezer until completely frozen.
2. Take a large jug, place half of the mint leaves into it, add the quarters of lime.
3. Use a rolling pin to crush the contents of the bowl until the juice and flavor are completely released.
4. Add lemonade and pomegranate juice to the bowl and mix well.
5. Take large cocktail glasses, add a couple of pomegranate ice cubes into each glass.
6. Pour the cocktail mixture evenly into each glass.
7. Add lime slices and the remaining mint for decoration.

CHAPTER 9

Martini Drinks

James Bond's 'Vesper' martini	37
Vodka Martini with Orange and Cardamom	37
James Bond's Favorite Cocktail-Vodka Martini	38
Passion Fruit Martini	38
Classic Pornstar Martini	38
Chocolate Egg Martini	38
Chocolate Orange Martini	39
Perfect Coffee Cocktail-Espresso Martini	39

James Bond's 'Vesper' martini

Prep Time: 5 minutes, Cook Time: 0, Serves: 1

INGREDIENTS:

60ml vodka

1 tbsp. vermouth, the dry version is best for this cocktail

The peel of a lemon for decoration

DIRECTIONS:

1. Take out a jug, add vermouth, vodka and some ice into it and stir well.
2. Pour into the cocktail shaker and shake it a few times.
3. Strain the cocktail into a martini glass.
4. Lemon zest for decoration.

Vodka Martini with Orange and Cardamom

Prep Time: 25 minutes, Cook Time: 0, Serves: 1

INGREDIENTS:

12 cardamom pods

400ml vodka

6 tbsps. Seville orange marmalade

4 tbsps. lemon juice

125ml Cointreau

Ice cubes

DIRECTIONS:

1. Use a mortar to mash ½ cardamom pods.
2. Stir the vodka and jam in a pan over medium heat. Add crushed cardamom pods. Turn off the heat before the mixture starts to boil. Let stand for about ½ hour, then filter.
3. Add lemon juice and Cointreau, put in the refrigerator for a while.
4. Add jam, ice cubes, and extra cardamom pods.

James Bond's Favorite Cocktail-Vodka Martini

Prep Time: 10 minutes, Cook Time: 0, Serves: 2

INGREDIENTS:

60ml (2 oz.) vodka
1 tbsp. dry vermouth
Ice cubes
Lemon peel, to garnish
1 olive, to garnish

DIRECTIONS:

1. Take a shaker, add the dry vermouth vodka and some ice, give it a few good shakes.
2. Take a chilled martini glass, pour the drink into it.
3. Add an olive on a cocktail stick or some lemon peel for decoration.

Classic Pornstar Martini

Prep Time: 10 minutes, Cook Time: 0, Serves: 2

INGREDIENTS:

the seeds of 1 passion fruit
1 ripe passion fruit, to serve
30ml passoa
1 tbsp. lime juice
60ml vanilla vodka
1 tbsp. sugar syrup
Prosecco, to serve

DIRECTIONS:

1. Take a cocktail shaker, add the passion fruit seeds into it.
2. Add the passoa, lime juice, vodka, and sugar syrup, along with ice. Shack well.
3. Take 2 martini glasses, pour the cocktail into it.
4. Top the glass up with prosecco, and add ½ passion fruit for decoration.

Passion Fruit Martini

Prep Time: 5 minutes, Cook Time: 0, Serves: 2

INGREDIENTS:

2 passion fruits, cut into halves
60ml vanilla flavoured vodka
1 tbsp. fresh lime juice
30ml quality passoa
Prosecco for serving
1 tbsp. sugar syrup
Handful of ice cubes

DIRECTIONS:

1. Prepare passion fruit, remove the seeds and skins, and leave the seeds on one side.
2. Take a cocktail shaker and add seeds.
3. Add passoa, vodka, syrup lime juice, and a few ice cubes, shake well.
4. Use a strainer to pour the drink into two martini glasses.
5. Add a little prosecco to the top.
6. Add half a passion fruit to each glass. Serve.

Chocolate Egg Martini

Prep Time: 15 minutes, Cook Time: 0, Serves: 1

INGREDIENTS:

25g mini chocolate eggs
25ml Baileys
25ml crème de cacao
50ml vodka
1 tsp. honey
Ice cubes

DIRECTIONS:

1. Take a plate, crush the chocolate eggs.
2. Brush some honey on the edge of the glass, and then dip it into the crushed chocolate.
3. Chill the glass for 2 hours.
4. Take a cocktail shaker, add Baileys, crème de cacao, vodka and ice cubes into it. Shake well.
5. Pour the cocktail into the chilled glass.

Chocolate Orange Martini

Prep Time: 15 minutes, Cook Time: 15 minutes, Serves: 4

INGREDIENTS:

100g golden caster sugar

The zest of 1 orange

Grated dark chocolate

100ml vodka

100ml crème de cacao

60ml orange syrup

40ml orange juice

Ice cubes

DIRECTIONS:

1. Mix the golden caster sugar and orange zest with 100ml of water and bring to a boil. Stir well until you get a smooth texture.
2. Chill four glasses. Once ready, dip the edges into grated dark chocolate.
3. Take a cocktail shaker, add the remaining liquid ingredients, orange juice, and some ice into it. Shake well.
4. Pour the cocktail into the glass and serve.

Perfect Coffee Cocktail-Espresso Martini

Prep Time: 20 minutes, Cook Time: 0, Serves: 2

INGREDIENTS:

100g golden caster syrup

100ml vodka

50ml freshly brewed espresso

50ml coffee liqueur

A few coffee beans, to garnish

DIRECTIONS:

1. Boil the caster sugar in 50ml (1.7 oz (47.6g)) of water. Let the mixture cool, stirring often, until the consistency is suitable for the syrup.
2. Take a cocktail shaker, pour 1 tbsp of this sugar into it with all other ingredients. Shake well.
3. Take 2 refrigerated martini glasses, pour the cocktail into it.
4. Add additional coffee beans for decoration.

CHAPTER 10

Cocktail Punch

Savory Berry Punch	41
Refreshing Caribbean Rum Punch	41
Non-alcoholic Punch	42
Rose Wine and Peach Punch	42
Fruity Vodka Punch	43
Refreshing Melon Cucumber Punch	43
Boozy Punch with Coconut Milk	43
Tropical Fruit Punch	43
Cucumber Vodka Punch	44

Savory Berry Punch

Prep Time: 5 minutes, Cook Time: 0, Serves: 10

INGREDIENTS:

350ml dark rum

1 litre of chilled ginger ale

1 litre of chilled cranberry juice

Ice cubes

DIRECTIONS:

1. Add the cranberry juice and ginger ale into a large punch bowl, stir carefully until everything is combined.
2. Add rum and combine once more.
3. Pour into cocktail glasses and top with plenty of ice cubes.

Refreshing Caribbean Rum Punch

Prep Time: 5 minutes, Cook Time: 0, Serves: 2

INGREDIENTS:

175ml fresh orange juice

75ml fresh lime juice

50ml sugar syrup

150ml rum, golden rum works well with this cocktail

A little grated nutmeg

A little grenadine syrup

A little Angostura bitters

A handful of ice cubes

A few orange slices for decoration

2 maraschino cherries for decoration

DIRECTIONS:

1. Add the orange and lime juices, sugar syrup, Angostura bitters, grenadine and rum to a mixing jug. Stir carefully until everything is combined.
2. Place the jug in the refrigerator for one hour.
3. Divide the drink between two cocktail glasses evenly.
4. Sprinkle a little nutmeg over the top of each glass.
5. Decorate with an orange slice and a cherry to each glass.

Non-alcoholic Punch

Prep Time: 20 minutes, Cook Time: 0, Serves: 8

INGREDIENTS:

100g cranberry

500ml blood orange juice

The juice of 1 lime

100ml cranberry juice

Lime wedges

Orange wedges

Mint sprigs

600ml Appletiser

DIRECTIONS:

1. Take a freezer container, put the cranberries into it, cover with water, freeze until solid.
2. Take a jar, put the orange juice, lime juice, and cranberry juice into it, mix well.
3. Take eight glasses, mash the frozen cranberries, and put them into it.
4. Add 1 lime, 1 orange, and some leaves to each glass.
5. Pour the mixed juice and top up the cocktail with Appletiser.

Rose Wine and Peach Punch

Prep Time: 15 minutes, Cook Time: 15 minutes, Serves: 1

INGREDIENTS:

The zest and juice 1½ lemon

4 tbsps. caster sugar

750ml rosé wine

150ml peach schnapps

1L soda water

½ lemon, sliced

1 peach, sliced

Ice cubes

DIRECTIONS:

1. In a saucepan, heat the lemon zest and sugar with 100ml of water. Leave to cool.
2. Take a jug, pour the mixture into it.
3. Add wine, gin and lemon juice. Stir well.
4. Add soda water, serve with ice cubes and fruits.

Fruity Vodka Punch

Prep Time: 15 minutes, Cook Time: 0, Serves: 1

INGREDIENTS:

- 50g caster sugar
- 125ml lemon juice
- 500ml apple juice
- 250ml vodka
- 250ml elderflower liqueur
- 125ml sparkling water
- Ice Cubes
- Lemon
- Fresh herbs, like mint and basil

DIRECTIONS:

1. Mix the sugar and lemon juice in a bowl. Stir well until the sugar is dissolved.
2. Transfer to a serving bowl along with all the other liquid ingredients.
3. Fill with ice cubes and stir once again.
4. Serve with lemon slices and herbs.

Boozy Punch with Coconut Milk

Prep Time: 5 minutes, Cook Time: 0, Serves: 4

INGREDIENTS:

- 25ml malibu
- 25ml tinned coconut milk
- 50ml fresh pineapple juice
- 50ml fresh mango juice
- A handful of ice cubes
- A few slices of pineapple for decoration

DIRECTIONS:

1. Add the ingredients into a large mixing jug, combing well.
2. Add some ice to each glass.
3. Pour the punch into each glass.
4. Add a slice of pineapple for decoration.

Refreshing Melon Cucumber Punch

Prep Time: 15 minutes, Cook Time: 0, Serves: 1

INGREDIENTS:

- 1 melon, cut in half
- 750ml white wine
- 50ml orange liqueur
- The juice of 1 lemon
- 100ml Pimm's
- 300ml sparkling water
- ½ cucumber, sliced
- 1 mint sprig
- Ice cubes

DIRECTIONS:

1. Take a large punch bowl, use a melon baller to cut the melon into balls.
2. Add white wine, orange liqueur, lemon juice and Pimm's. Chill for 2 hours.
3. Top with soda water and ice cubes.
4. Add mint sprigs and cucumber slices before serving.

Tropical Fruit Punch

Prep Time: 10 minutes, Cook Time: 0, Serves: 8

INGREDIENTS:

- 2 fresh rings of pineapple, chopped into pieces
- 1 peeled kiwi fruit, chopped into pieces
- A few strawberries, cut into halves
- Sparkling apple juice to taste
- Fruit juice to taste
- Soda water to taste
- A handful of ice cubes

DIRECTIONS:

1. Take a large mixing bowl and combine the kiwi fruit, pineapple pieces, and strawberries.
2. Take 8 large glasses, add a little of the fruit mixture to each one.
3. Add equal measurements of the tropical juice, apple juice, and a little soda water into the glasses.
4. Add a few ice cubes and serve.

Cucumber Vodka Punch

Prep Time: 20 minutes, Cook Time: 0, Serves: 1

INGREDIENTS:

1 small bunch mint, without leaves

1 large cucumber, chopped

500ml vodka

200g white caster sugar

1 small melon

The juice of 6 limes

1L sparkling water

Lime wedges

DIRECTIONS:

1. Take a jug, put half the mint and cucumber into it. Pour over your vodka. Cover and refrigerate for at least 24 hours. Once ready, use a strainer to pour the mixture.
2. Add cucumber, mint-infused vodka and sugar into a jug and stir well.
3. Using a melon squeezer, scoop out some melon balls and put them in the jug. Soak in the refrigerator for ½ hour.
4. Add soda water.
5. Add lime wedges and mint leaves for decoration.

CHAPTER 11

Vodka Drinks

Sex on The Beach	46
Hot Chocolate Vodka Shots	46
Vodka Cranberry Orange Cocktail	47
Orange Vodka with Chocolate	47
Eastern Breeze Vodka	48
Prosecco and Vodka Cocktail	48
Ginger Vodka with Apple	48
Vodka Prosecco Cocktail	48
Rhubarb Vodka Cocktail	49
Lemon and Thyme Vodka Cocktail	49

Sex on The Beach

Prep Time: 5 minutes, Cook Time: 0, Serves: 2

INGREDIENTS:

50ml vodka

25ml schnapps, peach works best

50ml fresh cranberry juice

The juice of 2 oranges

A handful of ice cubes

DIRECTIONS:

1. Prepare two tall cocktail glasses and add ice cubes separately.
2. Take out a large jug and add 50ml vodka, schnapps, cranberry, and orange juice into it, stir the mixtures until they are well mixed together.
3. Pour the cocktail evenly into the glass and stir carefully.
4. Add a few slices of oranges for decoration.

Hot Chocolate Vodka Shots

Prep Time: 15 minutes, Cook Time: 10 minutes, Serves: 6

INGREDIENTS:

1 tsp. chocolate spread

150ml vodka

75ml hazelnut liqueur

75ml chocolate cream liqueur

Ice cubes

2 packs of Kinder Bueno

DIRECTIONS:

1. In the microwave, heat the chocolate spread.
2. Take out six shot glasses, brush a line of chocolate inside them.
3. Take a cocktail shaker, add all the liquid ingredients and ice into it. Shake well.
4. Use a strainer to pour the cocktail into the shot glasses.
5. Add drink with Kinder Bueno chunks for decoration.

Vodka Cranberry Orange Cocktail

Prep Time: 10 minutes, Cook Time: 0, Serves: 12

INGREDIENTS:

200ml vodka Cointreau

200ml vodka

400ml orange juice

600ml cranberry juice

Crushed ice

Lime peel

DIRECTIONS:

1. Take a jug, put the Cointreau and the vodka into it.
2. Add orange and cranberry juices, stir the mixtures until they are well mixed together.
3. Take 12 glasses, fill them with cocktails and some crushed ice.
4. Add some with lime peel for decoration.

Orange Vodka with Chocolate

Prep Time: 25 minutes, Cook Time: 0, Serves: 4

INGREDIENTS:

100ml vodka

60ml orange liqueur

100ml creme de cacao

40ml fresh orange juice

The zest of 1 large orange

100g caster sugar

100ml cold water

A little dark chocolate, grated, for decoration

A handful of ice cubes

DIRECTIONS:

1. In a small saucepan, add water, sugar and orange zest into it and bring to a boil, stirring regularly.
2. Let the syrup cool and use a strainer to pour it into a small bowl.
3. Take 4 cocktail glasses, slightly moisten the rim of the glasses, and then dip them into grated chocolate for decoration. Put on the side.
4. Add cocoa cream, vodka, orange juice and freshly made dyeing syrup into a cocktail shaker.
5. Add ice cubes and give it a few good shakes.
6. Pour into the prepared glass.

Eastern Breeze Vodka

Prep Time: 10 minutes, Cook Time: 0, Serves: 6

INGREDIENTS:

Ice cubes

300ml vodka

600ml apple juice

Mint leaves

The seeds from 1 pomegranate

DIRECTIONS:

1. Take six wine glasses, fill them with ice cubes.
2. Add vodka and apple juice.
3. Add mint leaves and pomegranate seeds for decoration.

Prosecco and Vodka Cocktail

Prep Time: 15 minutes, Cook Time: 0, Serves: 4

INGREDIENTS:

The juice of 1 lemon

The juice of 1 orange

100ml vodka

25ml ginger beer or cordial

300ml Prosecco

A few hibiscus flower, including the syrup

A handful of ice cubes

DIRECTIONS:

1. In a cocktail shaker, add lemon juice, orange juice, vodka, ginger and a little ice into it and mix well.
2. Take 4 champagne glasses and add a hibiscus flower inside each one.
3. Strain the cocktail into each glass, leaving space for the Prosecco.
4. Add a little Prosecco to each glass.
5. Top with a teaspoon of the hibiscus syrup.

Ginger Vodka with Apple

Prep Time: 10 minutes, Cook Time: 0, Serves: 10

INGREDIENTS:

500ml vanilla flavoured vodka

1 litre ginger beer

500ml apple juice

The juice of 2 limes

2 limes sliced into wedges

A small piece of peeled and sliced ginger

1 thinly sliced apple

DIRECTIONS:

1. Take out a large jug, add all the liquid ingredients into it and stir well.
2. Add ginger, wedges of lime and apple, to the pot and mix them together.
3. Pour the cocktail into a glass and add extra ice cubes.

Vodka Prosecco Cocktail

Prep Time: 15 minutes, Cook Time: 0, Serves: 1

INGREDIENTS:

200ml vodka

400ml apple juice

750ml prosecco

The juice of 2 lemons

Ice cubes

1 lemon, sliced

1 apple, cored and finely sliced

DIRECTIONS:

1. Take a punch bowl, pour vodka, lemon and apple juice into it. Put it in the refrigerator for 2 hours.
2. Take a glass, pour the mixture into it and top with the Prosecco.
3. Add ice cubes.
4. Add lemon slices and apple slices for decoration.

Rhubarb Vodka Cocktail

Prep Time: 15 minutes, Cook Time: 25 minutes, Serves: 4

INGREDIENTS:

85g caster sugar

300g rhubarb, chopped

100ml vodka

75ml lemonade

30ml advocaat

1 rhubarb

DIRECTIONS:

1. Heat the sugar with 75ml water. Stir in the chopped rhubarb and bring to a boil. Cook until the rhubarb is very tender.
2. Take a bowl, pour the rhubarb mixture into it. Squeeze all the juices out of the rhubarb with a wooden spoon. Remove the mixture to the saucepan and stir over low heat until you get a syrupy mixture.
3. Take a jug, pour the mixture into it. At the same time, put 4 cocktail glasses in the refrigerator.
4. Take a cocktail shaker, add 2/3 of the rhubarb syrup, vodka and some ice cubes. Shake well.
5. Whisk the lemonade, adjuvant and ice cubes in another jug.
6. Take 4 chilled glasses, divide the rhubarb mixture into them. Add advocaat mixture on top.
7. Add extra rhubarb shreds for decoration.

Lemon and Thyme Vodka Cocktail

Prep Time: 15 minutes, Cook Time: 20 minutes, Serves: 8

INGREDIENTS:

8 lemons, halved

16 sprigs of thyme

1½ cups vodka

4 cups ice water

½ cup agave or simple syrup

Ice cubes

DIRECTIONS:

1. Prepare a grill, place the lemons on the grill over high heat until they are charred and soft. Squeeze the lime to get juice. While the lemons char, using tongs, hold 8 of the thyme sprigs over high heat just until they start to color and give off wisps of smoke.
2. Take a cocktail shaker, add the remaining 8 thyme sprigs, lemon juice, and ice cubes into it. Shake well.
3. Use a strainer to pour the mixture into a pitcher. Add the ice water, vodka, and agave, and stir until the agave is dissolved.
4. Take glasses, fill with ice cubes and pour the drinks into it.
5. Add a charred thyme sprig for decoration.

CHAPTER 12

For the Love of Wines

Easy Frozen Strawberry Daiquiri	51
Non-Alcoholic Mulled Wine	51
Apple Mulled Wine	52
Sangria with Red wine	52
Frozen Strawberry Daiquiri	53
Mulled Wine with Clementine	53

Easy Frozen Strawberry Daiquiri

Prep Time: 10 minutes, Cook Time: 0, Serves: 2

INGREDIENTS:

500g strawberries

100ml rum

The juice of ½ lime

200g ice

Lime slices, to garnish

1 strawberry, halved, to garnish

DIRECTIONS:

1. Place the strawberries in a blender, blend until you get a creamy texture, and remove all seeds.
2. Add rum, lime juice, and ice into it.
3. Take two glasses of martini, divide the mixed mixture into each one.
4. Add lime slices and half a strawberry for decoration.

Non-Alcoholic Mulled Wine

Prep Time: 20 minutes, Cook Time: 0, Serves: 6

INGREDIENTS:

500ml fresh pomegranate juice

A few blackberries, either fresh or frozen

250ml fresh apple juice

25g caster sugar

4 cloves

1 stick of cinnamon

1 star anise

1 orange, cut into quarters

3 black peppercorns

A few slices of orange for decoration

DIRECTIONS:

1. Take a large saucepan, combine the fresh pomegranate juice, blackberries, app juice, and sugar.
2. Add cloves, cinnamon stick, star anise, orange quarter, and peppercorns, stirring again.
3. Heat on low heat until the mixture starts to boil, stirring regularly.
4. Carefully test the mixture to see how it tastes. If you need it sweeter, add a little more sugar.
5. Once ready, remove the pan from the heat and use a strainer to pour the mixture into a heatproof glass.
6. Add a few orange slices for decoration.

Apple Mulled Wine

Prep Time: 15 minutes, Cook Time: 15 minutes, Serves: 1

INGREDIENTS:

1 apple juice

125ml red wine

115g caster sugar

1 cinnamon stick, halved

2 stars anise

3 tbsps. Cointreau

3 small apples, thinly sliced

100g frozen fruits

DIRECTIONS:

1. In a saucepan, combine the apple juice and wine.
2. Add cinnamon sticks, sugar, and star anise. Stir until the sugar dissolves, then cook for another 15 minutes.
3. Take a mug, pour the mixture into it. Add Cointreau, some apple slices and frozen fruit before serving.

Sangria with Red wine

Prep Time: 15 minutes, Cook Time: 0, Serves: 1

INGREDIENTS:

2 lemons, 1 chopped, 1 juiced

2 pears, chopped

2 oranges, chopped

200g red berries, chopped

1 tsp. cinnamon

3 tbsps. caster sugar

ice

750ml light red wine

100ml Spanish brandy

300ml sparkling water

DIRECTIONS:

1. Take a large bowl, put all the chopped fruit into it along with the cinnamon and sugar. Sir the mixtures until they are well mixed together.
2. Refrigerate at least for 1 hour.
3. Take a jar, fill it with ice cubes.
4. Add wine and brandy, stir the mixtures.
5. Top with soda water and serve.

Frozen Strawberry Daiquiri

Prep Time: 10 minutes, Cook Time: 0, Serves: 2

INGREDIENTS:

500g prepared strawberries

100ml rum

The juice of half a lime

200g ice

2 lime slices for decoration

DIRECTIONS:

1. Add the strawberries to a blender and blend down to a fine pulp.
2. After blending, take a small sieve and remove as many seeds from the berries as possible.
3. Place the strawberry mixture back to the blender and add the rum, lime juice, and the ice.
4. Then blend until combined and smooth.
5. Divide the mixture evenly between the two Martini glasses.
6. Use the lime slices to decorate the glass and drink whilst cold.

Mulled Wine with Clementine

Prep Time: 15 minutes, Cook Time: 20 minutes, Serves: 1

INGREDIENTS:

100g muscovado sugar

1 cinnamon stick

Additional star anise

4 cloves

150ml water

1 lemon

2 clementine

750ml light red wine

Orange zest

DIRECTIONS:

1. In a saucepan, heat 100g of sugar, one cinnamon stick, 1 star anise, cloves, and water. Bring to a boil and stir until the sugar dissolves.
2. Let the syrup simmer slowly, then transfer to a large jug and let it cool.
3. Add 1 lemon, 2 clementines, syrup, wine, and Cointreau. Stir well and chill for at least 2 hours.
4. Decorate the cocktail with ice cubes, a little orange peel, and extra star anise before serving.

CHAPTER 13

Gin Drinks

Sloe Gin with Lemon	55
Sweet Sloe Gin	55
Classic Gin Cocktail	56
Alcohol Free Gin & Tonic	56
Homemade Rhubarb Gin	57
Elderflower and Herbs Gin	57
Strawberry Gin	57
Spiced Apple Gin Cocktail	57
Classic Fizzy Gin	58
Apple and Elderflower Gin	58
Lemon and Rosemary Gin Sour	58
Gin with Elderflower	59
Campari, Gin and Pink Grapefruit	59

Sloe Gin with Lemon

Prep Time: 15 minutes, Cook Time: 0, Serves: 1

INGREDIENTS:

50ml sloe gin

25ml gin

25ml lemon juice

Ice cubes

Crushed ice

DIRECTIONS:

1. Boil the sugar with 100ml of water, then add juniper berries. Muddle with a spoon.
2. Add all the ingredients to the cocktail shaker and shake well, apart from crushed ice.
3. Take a tumbler, pour the cocktail into it and add crushed ice.

Sweet Sloe Gin

Prep Time: 15 minutes, Cook Time: 0, Serves: 1

INGREDIENTS:

1 tbsp. juniper berries

25ml gin

50ml sloe gin

25ml fresh lemon juice

100ml water

100g caster sugar

A handful of ice cubes

Crushed ice

DIRECTIONS:

1. Prepare a small saucepan, combining the sugar, water, and juniper berries.
2. Bring the pan to the boil and stir frequently.
3. Once boiling, remove the pan from the heat and mash the berries with a fork until they are completely liquid.
4. Place the pan on one side to cool down.
5. If you want to store the syrup for later use, strain it into a sterilized jar. You can keep this refrigerator for two weeks.
6. Take a cocktail shaker and add two types of gin, lemon juice, and 2 tsps. of juniper syrup.
7. Add a few ice cubes and give it a few good shakes.
8. Add some crushed ice to the tumbler.
9. Strain the cocktail into the glass.

Classic Gin Cocktail

Prep Time: 5 minutes, Cook Time: 0, Serves: 1

INGREDIENTS:

50ml cardamom gin

3 cardamom pods

100ml tonic water

A handful of ice cubes

DIRECTIONS:

1. Take out a large glass, add the ice and cardamom gin into it.
2. Crush the cardamom pods until they open.
3. Add the pods and tonic water into the glass and combine well.
4. Add extra ice cubes if you prefer.

Alcohol Free Gin & Tonic

Prep Time: 10 minutes, Cook Time: 0, Serves: 6

INGREDIENTS:

5 cardamom pods

Half a fresh cucumber

1 teabag, chamomile works best

The zest of 1 lemon

Half a bunch of fresh rosemary

A small bunch of fresh mint leaves

5 cloves

Tonic water to taste

500ml cold water

A handful of ice cubes

DIRECTIONS:

1. Crush the cardamom pod to the bruise.
2. Cut the cucumber into thin slices.
3. Take a large jug, add cucumber and cardamom pods into it.
4. Add tea bags, lemon zest, rosemary, mint, and cloves.
5. Add 500ml cold water and stir well.
6. Put in the refrigerator for at least 2 hours.
7. When you are ready to serve, take a cup and add 50ml of the mixture.
8. Pour enough tonic water on top and bring the mixture to the top of the glass.
9. Add a few ice cubes and a little mint for decoration.

Homemade Rhubarb Gin

Prep Time: 10 minutes, Cook Time: 0, Serves: 1

INGREDIENTS:

1 kg pink rhubarb stalks

400g caster sugar

800ml gin

DIRECTIONS:

1. Wash the rhubarb, trim the stalks, and remove the base and all leaves.
2. Take a big jar, cut the rhubarb stalks into pieces, and put them in with the sugar.
3. Shake everything and let it sit overnight.
4. After about 24 hours, you can add gin and shake the mixture again.
5. Rest at least 4 weeks before serving.

Strawberry Gin

Prep Time: 15 minutes, Cook Time: 0, Serves: 10

INGREDIENTS:

400g of sliced strawberries

700ml gin

100g caster sugar

DIRECTIONS:

1. In a large mixing bowl, combine berries, gin, and sugar, stir well.
2. Pour the mixture into a sterilized jar and seal.
3. Put the jar in the refrigerator and stir quickly every few days, for no longer than three weeks' duration.
4. Once ready to serve, strain the cocktail into a glass and add extra ice cubes.

Elderflower and Herbs Gin

Prep Time: 10 minutes, Cook Time: 0, Serves: 4

INGREDIENTS:

150ml gin

150ml elderflower liqueur

50ml elderflower cordial

8 edible flowers

2 rosemary sprigs, leaves only

2 thyme sprigs, leaves only

330ml sparkling water

Ice cubes

DIRECTIONS:

1. Take an ice cubes tray, fill the holes with flowers, water and herbs. Leave in the freezer until frozen.
2. Take a large jug, pour gin, elderflower liqueur and elderflower cordial into it, add some ice cubes. Stir well.
3. Take 4 tall glasses, pour the cocktail into it.
4. Top the glass up with soda and add some floral ice cubes for decoration.

Spiced Apple Gin Cocktail

Prep Time: 15 minutes, Cook Time: 0, Serves: 2

INGREDIENTS:

50ml gin

4 tbsps. apple juice

The juice of 1 lemon

Ground cinnamon

Ice cubes

200ml bottle sparkling wine

½ small apple, thinly sliced

DIRECTIONS:

1. Take a cocktail shaker, pour the gin into it.
2. Add apple juice, lemon juice, cinnamon and ice cubes. Shake well.
3. Take 2 fluted glasses, pour the mixture into each glass.
4. Add sparkling wine.
5. Top with extra cinnamon. Add apple slices for decoration.

Classic Fizzy Gin

Prep Time: 5 minutes, Cook Time: 0, Serves: 1

INGREDIENTS:

50ml gin

25ml fresh lemon juice

A little sparkling water

2 tsps. sugar syrup

A handful of ice cubes

A slice of lemon to decorate

DIRECTIONS:

1. Prepare a cocktail shaker, combine all the ingredients, apart from the lemon slices.
2. Fill the shaker up with the ice cubes and give it a few good shakes until the outside feels frosty.
3. Strain the cocktail into a glass.
4. Add a bit more ice and lemon slices for decoration.

Apple and Elderflower Gin

Prep Time: 10 minutes, Cook Time: 0, Serves: 8

INGREDIENTS:

200ml elderflower cordial

250ml gin

1L apple juice

Apple slices, to garnish

Ice cubes, to garnish

DIRECTIONS:

1. Take a mixing jug, add cordial and gin into it, mix well.
2. Take 8 glasses, pour the cocktail into each one.
3. Top the glass up with apple juice.
4. Add apple slices and some ice cubes for decoration.

Lemon and Rosemary Gin Sour

Prep Time: 15 minutes, Cook Time: 15 minutes, Serves: 4

INGREDIENTS:

8 sprigs of rosemary

¾ cup gin

¼ cup simple syrup

6 tbsps. freshly squeezed lemon juice

Ice cubes

Lemon slices, plain or grilled

DIRECTIONS:

1. Prepare a grill, use tongs to burn the rosemary on the grill at high heat until the leaves start to smoke.
2. Take four rock glasses, fill them with ice cubes, put one stick in each glass.
3. Take a cocktail shaker, add the remaining sticks, gin, lemon juice, simple syrup, and ice cubes into it. Shake well.
4. Use a strainer to pour the mixture into a glass.
5. Add lemon slices for decoration.

Gin with Elderflower

Prep Time: 20 minutes, Cook Time: 0, Serves: 1

INGREDIENTS:

1 cucumber

100ml gin

100ml elderflower cordial

Tonic water

DIRECTIONS:

1. Take a bowl, grate the cucumber using the large holes in a box grater, and then squeeze out all the juice with a spoon.
2. Add the gin and elderflower cordial.
3. Take a glass, pour the cocktail into it.
4. Top the glass up with tonic water.
5. Serve with cucumber strips.

Campari, Gin and Pink Grapefruit

Prep Time: 10 minutes, Cook Time: 0, Serves: 1

INGREDIENTS:

750ml rose wine

100ml gin

50ml Campari

25ml red vermouth

200ml pink grapefruit juice

1 tbsp. honey

Ice cubes

½ bunch of thyme

DIRECTIONS:

1. Take a punch bowl, add all the ingredients into it.
2. Add ice and stir carefully until everything is combined.
3. Add thyme for decoration.

CHAPTER 14

Fruity Cocktails

Strawberry Champagne Cocktail	61
Caipirinhas with Pineapple	61
Blood Orange with Grand Marnier	62
Salted Caramel Pecan and Clementine	62
Sweet Blood Orange Bourbon Cocktail	63
Bloody Mary Cocktail	63
Citrus and Aperol Cocktail	64
Cranberry Cocktail with Lemonade	64
Watermelon Lime Spritzer	64
Orange Cocktail-Tequila Sunrise	64
Rhubarb Orange Mocktail	65
Mint Berry Mocktail	65
Non-Alcoholic- Peach Long Island Iced Tea	66

Strawberry Champagne Cocktail

Prep Time: 15 minutes, Cook Time: 0, Serves: 1

INGREDIENTS:

100g strawberries

50g caster sugar

2 tbsps. rosewater

Champagne

DIRECTIONS:

1. Place strawberries, sugar and rosewater in a blender and process until you get a puree.
2. Take a cocktail glass, pour the cocktail into it.
3. Add Champagne and serve.

Caipirinhas with Pineapple

Prep Time: 15 minutes, Cook Time: 0, Serves: 8

INGREDIENTS:

1 pineapple, cut into chunks

A few sprigs of mint

The juice of 4 limes

8 tbsps. caster sugar

400ml light rum

800ml fresh pineapple juice

Crushed ice

DIRECTIONS:

1. Add around half the pineapple chunks, mint, lime juice, and sugar into a large pitcher.
2. Mash the mixture down into a pulp with a rolling pin.
3. Add the rum and combine it with the pulp.
4. Add the pineapple juice to the top of the pitcher.
5. Pour the cocktail into 8 glasses equally and add some crushed ice into each.
6. Decorate the glasses with any left-over pineapple.

Blood Orange with Grand Marnier

Prep Time: 20 minutes, Cook Time: 30 minutes, Serves: 1

INGREDIENTS:

4 blood oranges, quartered

120ml Grand Marnier

4 tsps. tequila

1 star anise

Prosecco

DIRECTIONS:

1. Soak the blood orange in the Grand Marnier for 3 hours. Save approximately 20ml of Grand Mardier for later use.
2. Place the oranges and their soaking liquid in an oven at 400 F (205ºC) and roast them with star anise for 30 minutes.
3. Take out the star anise and orange peel, put the fruit in a food processor and puree it.
4. Take a mixing jug, combine part of the fruit puree, Tequila and Grand Marnier.
5. Take a glass, add prosecco and pour the mixture into it.

Salted Caramel Pecan and Clementine

Prep Time: 20 minutes, Cook Time: 0, Serves: 2

INGREDIENTS:

100g toasted pecans, chopped

160g golden caster sugar

120ml clementine juice

3 egg whites

Vodka

½ tsp. sea salt flakes

18 drops chocolate bitters

Ice cubes

6 dehydrated orange slices

Nutmeg powder

DIRECTIONS:

1. Heat the pecans, salt, and sugar with 80ml of water. Let cool, then pour through a sieve to separate the pecans.
2. Take a cocktail shaker, add the clementine juice, egg whites, vodka, pecan salt and caramel syrup into it. Shake well until the egg whites gains volume.
3. Add ice cubes and shake for another 15 seconds.
4. Use a strainer to pour the drink into coupe glasses.
5. Add dehydrated orange slices and fresh nutmeg for decoration.

Sweet Blood Orange Bourbon Cocktail

Prep Time: 20 minutes, Cook Time: 20 minutes, Serves: 4

INGREDIENTS:

4 blood oranges

¾ cup bourbon

1 tbsp. sugar, plus more for rimming the glasses

ice cubes

DIRECTIONS:

1. Prepare a grill for high heat. Cut 3 oranges in half, cut side down, grill until charred. Cut the remaining oranges into thick slices, and roast them until both sides are browned, set aside.
2. Squeeze the orange to get 1 cup of juice.
3. Take a cocktail shaker, add juice, bourbon, sugar and ice cubes into it. Shake well for about 30 seconds.
4. Use a strainer to pour the cocktail into martini glasses.
5. Decorate with burnt orange slices.

Bloody Mary Cocktail

Prep Time: 5 minutes, Cook Time: 0, Serves: 2

INGREDIENTS:

500ml tomato juice

1 tbsp. fresh lemon juice

100ml vodka

Tabasco sauce to taste

Worcestershire sauce to taste

A little black pepper to taste

A handful of ice cubes

2 sticks of celery for decoration

DIRECTIONS:

1. In a large kettle, add ice cubes.
2. Add tomato juice, lemon juice, vodka, two sauces, and a little pepper according to your taste. Stir the mixtures until the outer side of the jug is cold.
3. Strain the cocktail into 2 tall glasses.
4. Add a few ice cubes and a stick of celery for garnish.

Citrus and Aperol Cocktail

Prep Time: 5 minutes, Cook Time: 0, Serves: 4

INGREDIENTS:

300ml fresh orange juice
200ml Aperol
100ml limoncello
100ml vodka
1 tbsp. triple sec
Orange slices for decoration

DIRECTIONS:

1. Prepare a mixing jug, add all the ingredients except orange slices into it, stir well.
2. Pour the cocktail into 4 glasses and add ice to each.
3. Garnish with orange slices.

Watermelon Lime Spritzer

Prep Time: 10 minutes, Cook Time: 0, Serves: 8

INGREDIENTS:

2 limes, cut into pieces
100g watermelon, chopped
2 tbsps. gin
Tonic water

DIRECTIONS:

1. Take 8 cocktail glasses, squeeze a few slices of lime into it, and then drop in the flesh.
2. Divide the watermelon slices into glasses.
3. Add some ice cubes and gin.
4. Top the glasses up with tonic water.

Cranberry Cocktail with Lemonade

Prep Time: 10 minutes, Cook Time: 0, Serves: 4

INGREDIENTS:

4 oz. (113 g) cranberry-raspberry juice
4 oz. (113 g) vodka
4 oz. (113 g) thawed lemonade concentrate
4 oz. (113 g) peach schnapps liqueur
16 maraschino cherries

DIRECTIONS:

1. Prepare a shaker, fill three-quarters of it with ice cubes.
2. Add vodka, concentrated lemonade, gin, and juice to the shaker; cover and shake for about 10-15 seconds until condensation forms on the outside of the shaker. Strain into four cocktail glasses. Place a skewer with four cherries in each glass.
3. Serve immediately.

Orange Cocktail-Tequila Sunrise

Prep Time: 10 minutes, Cook Time: 0, Serves: 1

INGREDIENTS:

2 tbsps. grenadine
50ml tequila
1 tbsp. triple sec
The juice of 1 orange
The juice of ½ lemon
Ice cubes
1 cocktail cherry

DIRECTIONS:

1. Take a tall glass, place the grenadine into the base of it.
2. Take a cocktail shaker, put the triple sec, tequila, fruit juices, and ice into it. Shake well.
3. Add ice cubes to the tall glass and then use a strainer to pour the cocktail into it.
4. Add a cherry on a cocktail stick for decoration.

Rhubarb Orange Mocktail

Prep Time: 20 minutes, Cook Time: 0, Serves: 10

INGREDIENTS:

300g caster sugar

The juice and zest of 1 orange

The juice and zest of 1 lemon

300ml water

1 peeled slice of root ginger, fresh

450g fresh, chopped rhubarb

Sparkling water to taste

A handful of ice cubes

DIRECTIONS:

1. Add water and sugar into a large saucepan.
2. Simmer the mixture until the sugar dissolves.
3. Add orange zest and juice, then add lemon zest juice and stir.
4. Add ginger and rhubarb and mix again.
5. Cook over medium-low heat and stir regularly until the rhubarb starts to soften and crack.
6. Remove the pan from the heat, strain the mixture into a heat-resistant measuring jug.
7. Transfer the mixture to a sterilized jar. This mixture can be stored in the refrigerator for up to 4 weeks.
8. When you are ready to serve, take a cocktail glass and add a handful of ice to the bottom.
9. Pour 25ml of rhubarb mixture into a glass, add soda water according to personal taste.

Mint Berry Mocktail

Prep Time: 15 minutes, Cook Time: 0, Serves: 1

INGREDIENTS:

120ml sparkling lemonade

200ml water

1 sprig of fresh mint, chopped

1 fresh cucumber, cut into small pieces

A handful of red berries, either fresh or frozen

A handful of ice cubes

A few slices of orange and lime for decoration

DIRECTIONS:

1. Take a small saucepan, add mint, cucumber slices, and 200ml of water, and boil.
2. Stir until combined and remove from heat.
3. Add the berries and make them soft, then crush and squash everything with a fork.
4. After cooling down completely, use a strainer to pour the mixture into a bowl.
5. Take a tall glass, add 40ml of the mixture.
6. Add a few ice cubes and add lemonade to the top of the glass and stir gently.
7. Add oranges and lime slices for decoration.

Non-Alcoholic- Peach Long Island Iced Tea

Prep Time: 15 minutes, Cook Time: 0, Serves: 12

INGREDIENTS:

200g sugar

250ml water

4 peaches with stones removed, chopped into pieces

2 litres of boiling water

4 regular teabags

Plenty of ice cues

1 sliced peach for decoration

DIRECTIONS:

1. Add sugar and 150ml water into a medium pan.
2. Heat to a boil, stir until the sugar is completely dissolved.
3. Add the peaches and continue to stir, cook until the peaches are soft.
4. Remove the pan from the heat and mash the peaches with the back of the fork.
5. Leave on one side for one hour.
6. When ready, sift the syrup to remove any small or large pieces.
7. Mash the mixture into a puree.
8. Take a large glass mixing pot, add tea bags, and pour 2 liters of boiling water on it.
9. Set on one side for 4 minutes, stir and remove the tea bag, and drain it.
10. Let the tea cool, then put it in the refrigerator.
11. Take a tall glass, pour half of the peach syrup and ice tea.
12. Add some ice cubes, or if you like, you can also add a little soda.
13. Add peach slices for decoration.

CHAPTER 15

Special Cocktails

Modern Classic Cocktail-Mai Tai	68
New York Sour	68
Singapore Sling Cocktail	69
Long Island Iced Tea Cocktail	69
Classic Brazilian Caipirinha	70
Easy Pimm's Cup Cocktail	70
Sour Cocktail-Sidecar	70
Simple Negroni Cocktail	70
Classic Cuba Libre	71
Mai Tai Cocktail	71
Cynar Spritz	71
Easy WOO WOO Cocktail	71
Easy Pink Negroni	72
Negroni Cocktail	72
Italian Bicyclette	73
New York Sour Cocktail	73

Modern Classic Cocktail-Mai Tai

Prep Time: 10 minutes, Cook Time: 0, Serves: 1

INGREDIENTS:

2 tbsps. white rum

2 tbsps. dark rum

2 tbsps. triple sec

1 tbsp. grenadine

1 tbsp. almond syrup

The juice of ½ lime

1 maraschino cherry

ice cubes

DIRECTIONS:

1. Take a cocktail shaker, add all the ingredients into it and mix well.
2. Take a tumbler, add ice cubes and pour the cocktail into it.
3. Add a cherry for decoration before serving.

New York Sour

Prep Time: 10 minutes, Cook Time: 0, Serves: 1

INGREDIENTS:

50ml rye whiskey

2 tsps. maple syrup

A dash of bitter orange

1 tbsp. egg white

25ml fresh lemon juice

A handful of ice cubes

20ml red wine

DIRECTIONS:

1. Take a cocktail shaker and add the whiskey, maple syrup, orange bitters, and lemon juice. Stir carefully until everything is combined.
2. Place the egg white onto a small plate and stir quickly with a spoon to loosen up.
3. Take a shaker, pour the egg white into it and give it a few shakes.
4. Add some ice cubes and shake once more, until the outside feels cold.
5. Strain the mixture into the serving glass, leaving a little space at the top.
6. Fill up the rest of the glass with the red wine.

Singapore Sling Cocktail

Prep Time: 5 minutes, Cook Time: 0, Serves: 1

INGREDIENTS:

25ml cherry brandy

25ml Benedictine

25ml gin

25ml fresh lime juice

50ml fresh pineapple juice

Angostura bitters to taste

Sparkling water to taste

Glace cherries to decorate

A handful of ice cubes

DIRECTIONS:

1. Take a large jug, combine the brandy, Benedictine, and the gin.
2. Add the ice and the bitters, stir until the outer edge of the glass feels icy.
3. Take a tall cocktail glass, add the lime, pineapple juices and the alcohol mixture. Stir carefully.
4. Top the glass up with the sparkling water.
5. Garnish with the cherry.

Long Island Iced Tea Cocktail

Prep Time: 5 minutes, Cook Time: 0, Serves: 4

INGREDIENTS:

50ml vanilla flavoured vodka

50ml gin

50ml tequila

50ml rum

50ml triple sec

100ml lime juice

500ml cola

A handful of ice cubes

Lime wedges for decoration

DIRECTIONS:

1. In a large jug, add alcoholic beverages.
2. Add lime juice, cola and top up to halfway with ice cubes. Stir well.
3. Add lime cubes.
4. Divide the cocktail into 4 tall glasses and pour more ice cubes. Serve.

Classic Brazilian Caipirinha

Prep Time: 10 minutes, Cook Time: 0, Serves: 1

INGREDIENTS:

2 limes, chopped into wedges

6 tsps. golden caster sugar

200ml cachaça

Crushed ice

Additional lime wedges, to garnish

DIRECTIONS:

1. Take a jug, put the sugar and the lime wedges in it. Use a blender or wooden spoon to mash everything up to make sure the lime releases as much juice as possible.
2. Take a cocktail glass, pour the syrup and the cachaça into it. Top the glass up with ice and extra lime wedges.

Sour Cocktail-Sidecar

Prep Time: 10 minutes, Cook Time: 0, Serves: 1

INGREDIENTS:

50ml cognac

25ml triple sec

25ml lemon juice

Angostura bitters

Ice cubes

DIRECTIONS:

1. Put a couple of glasses in the refrigerator for several hours.
2. Take a cocktail shaker, put all the ingredients into it.
3. Shake the cocktail well, then pour it into the refrigerated coupe glass.
4. Add a dash of Angostura bitters.

Easy Pimm's Cup Cocktail

Prep Time: 10 minutes, Cook Time: 0, Serves: 1

INGREDIENTS:

200ml Pimm's No. 1

600ml lemonade

Ice cubes

Fresh strawberries, to garnish

Sliced cucumber, to garnish

Sliced orange, to garnish

Mint sprigs, to garnish

DIRECTIONS:

1. Take a jug, fill it with Pimm's, ice, and lemonade.
2. Stir the mixtures until they are well mixed together.
3. Add strawberries, cucumber slices, orange slices, and mint sprigs for decoration.

Simple Negroni Cocktail

Prep Time: 5 minutes, Cook Time: 0, Serves: 1

INGREDIENTS:

25ml Campari

25ml gin

25ml vermouth, the sweet version works

well with this cocktail

A handful of ice cubes

A few orange slices for decoration

DIRECTIONS:

1. Prepare a mixing jug, combine the Campari, gin, and vermouth.
2. Add ice and stir until the outside of the container starts to feel icy.
3. Strain the drink into a tumbler glass.
4. Add some more ice and orange slices for decoration.

Classic Cuba Libre

Prep Time: 5 minutes, Cook Time: 0, Serves: 1

INGREDIENTS:

100ml (3.4 oz.(96.2 g)) cola

50ml (1.7 oz. (47.6 g)) white rum

Ice cubes

½ lime, cut into wedges

DIRECTIONS:

1. Take a tall glass, squeeze the juice from some of the lime wedges into it.
2. Fill it with ice.
3. Add the rum and the cola, and stir gently.
4. Add the remaining wedges into the glass before serving.

Cynar Spritz

Prep Time: 10 minutes, Cook Time: 0, Serves: 1

INGREDIENTS:

Ice cubes

30ml white wine

30ml Cynar

15ml crème de cassis

Soda water, to taste

1 sprig of thyme

DIRECTIONS:

1. Take a wine glass, fill it with ice cubes.
2. Pour in all your liquid ingredients. Stir gently until everything is combined.
3. Top with soda water.
4. Add the thyme for decoration before serving.

Mai Tai Cocktail

Prep Time: 5 minutes, Cook Time: 0, Serves: 1

INGREDIENTS:

2 tbsps. white rum

2 tbsps. dark rum

1 tbsp. almond syrup

Half a lime, juiced

1 tbsp. grenadine

2 tbsps. triple sec

A handful of ice cubs

1 maraschino cherry for decoration

DIRECTIONS:

1. Add all the ingredients into a cocktail shaker, except for the cherry and the ice cubes.
2. Add the ice cubes and shake until the outside is cold.
3. Take a tumbler glass, pour the cocktail into it.
4. Add maraschino cherry for decoration.

Easy WOO WOO Cocktail

Prep Time: 10 minutes, Cook Time: 0, Serves: 4

INGREDIENTS:

50ml (1.7 oz. (47.6g)) vodka

The juice of ½ lemon

100ml (3.4 oz. (96.8g)) cranberry juice

24ml (0.8 oz. (24.4g)) peach schnapps

Lime wedges

Ice cubes

DIRECTIONS:

1. Prepare a shaker, add all the liquid ingredients, lime juice and some ice cubes into the shaker and shake well.
2. Strain the cocktail into a glass and add extra ice cubes.
3. Garnish with lime wedges, serve.

Easy Pink Negroni

Prep Time: 10 minutes, Cook Time: 0, Serves: 1

INGREDIENTS:

15ml Aperol

35ml pink gin

25ml rose vermouth

Ice cubes

Some wedges of pink grapefruit, to garnish

1 basil leaf, to garnish

DIRECTIONS:

1. Take a tumbler, pour the Aperol, pink gin, and vermouth into it, add ice. Stir well.
2. Decorate with some pink grapefruit wedges and a basil leaf.

Negroni Cocktail

Prep Time: 20 minutes, Cook Time: 0, Serves: 1

INGREDIENTS:

Half a grapefruit

125g caster sugar

1 slice of fresh orange

3 crushed cardamom pods

A few coriander seeds

25ml grape juice, white grape juice is best for this cocktail

125ml water

25ml cold water

A handful of ice cubes

DIRECTIONS:

1. Cut the grapefruit into small chunks.
2. Take a medium saucepan, combine grapefruit, sugar, orange slices, cardamom pods, coriander seeds, and 125ml water.
3. Heat over medium heat until the mixture starts to boil. Once this happens, stir for 5 minutes on low heat.
4. After the fruit is completely soft and mushy, remove the pan from the fire.
5. Allow to cool.
6. Once the contents of the pan are cool, take a bowl and use a strainer to pour the mixture into it.
7. Take a glass and add some ice cubes.
8. Add 25ml of the strained syrup, grape juice, and 25ml of cold water to the glass.
9. Carefully stir the contents of the glass.
10. Serve when the outside of the glass feels cold.

Italian Bicyclette

Prep Time: 10 minutes, Cook Time: 0, Serves: 2

INGREDIENTS:

100ml Campari

200ml dry white wine

4-5 Ice cubes

½ lemon (sliced)

DIRECTIONS:

1. Take 2 glasses, pour the Campari into them.
2. Add a couple of ice cubes to each glass.
3. Top with white wine, stir well.
4. Add lemon wedges for decoration before serving.

New York Sour Cocktail

Prep Time: 10 minutes, Cook Time: 0, Serves: 1

INGREDIENTS:

50ml of strong tea

25ml fresh lemon juice

10ml fresh pomegranate juice

3 tsps. maple syrup

1 tbsp. egg white

A little vanilla extract to taste

A handful of ice cubes

DIRECTIONS:

1. Make up the tea and add the vanilla whilst it's still hot.
2. Set aside and let it cool.
3. Add the maple syrup, lemon juice and tea to a cocktail shaker.
4. Add the egg white and stir carefully to break up.
5. Shake the cocktail shaker until the mixture is frothy.
6. Add a handful of ice cubes to the shaker and combine once more, until the outside of the shaker is cold.
7. Add a little more ice to the cocktail glass.
8. Use a strainer to pour the mixture into the cocktail glass.
9. Take a small measuring jug and add the pomegranate juice, adding water until it reaches the 20ml mark.
10. Pour the pomegranate into the glass slowly.

CONCLUSION

Are you to some mixing and pouring? Well, now you have a complete range of cocktail recipes that you can practice at home or at the bar to master your bartending skills. The mixing techniques and the tips shared in the second chapter of this cookbook are there to help every newbie to understand the basics of bartending and how to manage the different tasks without messing things up. So, go ahead, give these cocktails a try and spread the joy around! Have a happy cocktail making!

Appendix : Measurement Conversion Chart

Volume Equivalents (Dry)

US STANDARD	METRIC (APPROXIMATE)
1/8 teaspoon	0.5 mL
1/4 teaspoon	1 mL
1/2 teaspoon	2 mL
3/4 teaspoon	4 mL
1 teaspoon	5 mL
1 tablespoon	15 mL
1/4 cup	59 mL
1/2 cup	118 mL
3/4 cup	177 mL
1 cup	235 mL
2 cups	475 mL
3 cups	700 mL
4 cups	1 L

Temperatures Equivalents

FAHRENHEIT (F)	CELSIUS(C) (APPROXIMATE)
225 °F	107 °C
250 °F	120 °C
275 °F	135 °C
300 °F	150 °C
325 °F	160 °C
350 °F	180 °C
375 °F	190 °C
400 °F	205 °C
425 °F	220 °C
450 °F	235 °C
475 °F	245 °C
500 °F	260 °C

Volume Equivalents (Liquid)

US STANDARD	US STANDARD (OUNCES)	METRIC (APPROXIMATE)
2 tablespoons	1 fl.oz.	30 mL
1/4 cup	2 fl.oz.	60 mL
1/2 cup	4 fl.oz.	120 mL
1 cup	8 fl.oz.	240 mL
1 1/2 cup	12 fl.oz.	355 mL
2 cups or 1 pint	16 fl.oz.	475 mL
4 cups or 1 quart	32 fl.oz.	1 L
1 gallon	128 fl.oz.	4 L

Weight Equivalents

US STANDARD	METRIC (APPROXIMATE)
1 ounce	28 g
2 ounces	57 g
5 ounces	142 g
10 ounces	284 g
15 ounces	425 g
16 ounces (1 pound)	455 g
1.5 pounds	680 g
2 pounds	907 g

Made in United States
North Haven, CT
18 December 2022

29551139R00044